What Colours a Pākehā

To Denis

Hope this makes up
for some of the yarns
we missed out on over
the years.

Fond regards
PADDY

What Colours a Pākehā

(Poetry and Prose)

by

Patrick Coogan

Earl of Seacliff Art Workshop
Paekakariki
2004

© Copyright Patrick Coogan, 2004

Cover illustration: Bridie Coogan

Printed at: Precise Print and Design, Paraparaumu

Published by:

    Earl of Seacliff Art Workshop

    P.O.Box 42

    Paekakariki

    email: pukapuka@paradise.net.nz

ISBN 1-86942-042-X

Contents

Foreword by Apirana Taylor

What Colours a Pākehā 9

Jazz Spring in Dunedin 11

Saying it Like it Is 24

Helping the Boss Out 28

The Poetry Reading 34

St. George and a Dragon 40

The White Horse Haka 46

Leaving School 49

Fish Webs 52

Cabbage Sunday 56

Confessions from a Rabbit Hunter 60

A Bush Night Out 64

In the Beef Market 71

The Ruru 80

Hunting Pigs 86

The Murupara Gig 94

Milk Cow Blues 98

He aint Heavy… 102

You can't go wrong with a Hāngi 105

A Grey Faced Smiling Suitman Said 110

Foreword

Patrick Coogan is a new and interesting writer, writing with a new voice, championing the underdog on an age-old landscape of oppression. He mixes humour and pain with his whiskey and beer as he writes.
His poem, **'What Colours a Pākehā'** is an important piece written with insight and understanding, looking into an area where few bother to look. Paddy and I have often walked similar paths together and crossed pens from time to time and so it is with pleasure I see his words take wing before a world that often strives to not understand.

Apirana Taylor

What Colours a Pākehā

Dedication

In loving memory of my parents
Jack Coogan and Ann Dooley who had the guts to get out.

To Mrs Stanley Roche, who first believed in me
and gave me the confidence to write.

And to Margaret who taught me to love.

What Colours a Pākehā

Pākehā come multi hued
not all labelled red, white and blue.
Historical discordance
coloured the tribal milieu.

Green was my colour,
as worn by the children of Tāne
on these newly forested hills.
Te Ariki sent a Celtic acorn
and planted me in a pūriri grove.

Ancestral spirit shaped me,
Papa adopted and suckled me.
My tekoteko
is as long as your tekoteko.
A koru unfurling,
cut off,
attaching to a new frond.

From a magic isle shrouded in mist
We heard the lament of the Irish pipes
Hail Mary's of weeping
For those
wrenched from our mother's womb.

The passionate joy of laughter and song
frothed ebullient as Guinness
dancing around the fires of our home.
We heard the tales of oppression and hunger,
chanted the rebel songs of defiance
that fostered the warrior spirit.

I walked to school with green cap
A symbol of the family coat of arms:
"Constans Fidei."
To others a beacon of scorn.
A catholic dog that stunk like a frog
A thick Irish Paddy
tattooed across my very name
I learned well that long nosed look of disdain

"You wouldn't be Irish would you?"

A tragic emptiness deep down
coming from a place
where you had never been.
Worse to be told
you didn't belong
In the only place
you'd ever seen.

I fought them.
A reluctant victim
trapped in the ancient struggle.
To admit that I
was second rate
a more crippling death.

Te Ariki placed a greenstone taonga
in the rivers of Aotearoa.
A sign for us
cleansed of ancient oppression.

Our treasure
realised in the freedom of God.
He placed the people of his choice
in this indulgent land.
To love justice and mercy
to learn the pattern of his hand.

Jazz Spring in Dunedin

I begin the childhood walk, crossing Queens Gardens opposite the NZR bus station. The weather sunny, slightly cool, with a light breeze. Traffic flows in lazy waves orchestrated by the lights. I walk gladly with emotive anticipation. I see Terry at thirteen, begging for money off gullible older women.
    "Please Mrs, my brother and I live at Ravensbourne and we have lost our bus fare."
Sometimes it worked and we bought hot chips, or pea pie and pud from the pie cart. On cold, drizzling nights we huddled against the heated radiators inside that bus station. An art deco treasure. Multi coloured marble pillars, ending in soft rounded curves, reflecting the shape of the Otago Harbour. A womb shaped slit with legs and breasted hills, enfolding on both sides. I was nurtured at the top of the left leg, at Ravensbourne, to where I walked on this spring morning. I hear the crystal voice of my Irish mother sing to me from the scone warmed kitchen.

If I was a blackbird I'd whistle and sing
And follow the ship that my true love sails in.
And there on the top rigging, I'd there build my nest
And pillow my head, on his lily white breast.

And we fell asleep well loved, in the bedroom with the fireplace, and the warm coats on the bed.
    That bus station was built in the days when bus travel was important and prestigious. Lift up luggage hatches of polished wood. The solid doors with glass panels, and NZR crest proudly displayed. The toilets are the very ones I had used forty years ago. I wondered again what secrets lay behind that door marked *ladies*.
    Today I walk with a spring in my step. Home to the place where that magic time of life was realised. I had often walked this route with my father when I accompanied him early, through the frost, to Mass and work. He told me stories of his adventures at sea, imbuing me with a love of narrative and adventure. He taught me whakapapa, painting the Coogan connection through Manchester to Kilkenny. He was a big man, with a long black coat, carrying his small leather suitcase with overalls, knives and aprons. He was chef at the Law Courts hotel. No one messed with my Dad. He was quick to laugh, fierce and carried a confident authority.
    Nee's corner where the furniture factory had been. We caught the Ravensbourne bus from there after school, when we went to Holy Name

convent. One afternoon, the two Wadray brothers were also waiting and started to hassle us. It was Roseanne, Jim and I, so being the oldest male the responsibility lay with me. I was ten, solid and average height. The youngest Wadray was eleven, the older brother thirteen. We were defending a delaying action when the old man drove past and noticed what was going on. He stopped the car and came over.

"Do you boys want a fight? Paddy'll fight you."
Thanks Dad I thought, but grimly put up my fists and circled the older Wadray boy. Obedience to my father, and family honour was stronger than my fear of a hiding. I would have fought with passionate desperation, after the initial fear was smashed out of me, with the first blow.

"Hang on a minute," said Dad, "you're a bit big, what about your brother?"
The brother was too scared to fight, so the day was a draw. The old man offered them a ride home, and we never had any more trouble from those Wadray boys.

I walk past the pole that wiped out 18 year old Arthur Sanderson. A youthful, impetuous bud, exploding with such vigour into death. He splattered his guts around that pole, taking the corner too fast on his BSA motor bike. Past the wool stores, where the old man worked, when he was on harder times. Lugging the bails with a hook. Sweating away for the export trade. Dunedin is a seaport. The harbour, blue green today, under a warming sun. A kererū swoops, mirroring the shape of the hills. The quarry tumbles a jagged edge into the sea. Past the fertiliser works, acrid bite. A whiff of haunting memories, pangs of violence and strife.

Ravensbourne begins for me at the monument, at the bottom of the zigzag. I sit awhile, examining the boat shed, picturing where the railway station had been. I crack out the thermos and drink hot coffee, seeing Roseanne meet me off the bus on winter evenings, to help me carry my piano accordion up the hill. For the sake of my mother, I learned to squeak out a second rate

hi die de deedle deedle didily idle de

and I wasn't too bad on

Hang down your head Tom Dooley.

My mother's people, are the Dooleys from Carrickmacross, just outside Dundalk. The monument, a squared obelisk. An erect penis, in memory of the men who ejaculated their life out on the battlefield, for the sake of that oppressive empire. For your gracious sake I shatter my world, annihilating the life and pride of a mother's son. Two 303 Lee Enfield rifles are carved in white stone. The listed dead contain two Dooleys. I rest before climbing the hill.

I walk up towards the top of the hill behind our place. The bush nestled beautifully in the dappled sunlight. Tuis collect noisily around the spring kōwhai nectar. Kererū flap lazily across the hill. I realise again why I rediscovered my soul among the bush of the Far North. That bush became my refuge, the source of nature's love. God of creation, lead me in the love of a caring father. On the way up the second zigzag I meet a Māori woman with her Pākehā mokopuna. We talk.

"I was brought up here, at 13 Matai St Ravensbourne."
She had only lived here 16 years and was clearly impressed. Being Māori she accepted the rights of turangawaewae. For once the boot was on the other foot. This was my land and I welcomed her to it. I blanketed her liberally with our Coogan mana, knowing that the oldest residents would still remember. Here I had laboured to build something of worth. Anyway, as a family we usually championed the underdog. Being the only Catholics in a Protestant street developed an empathy. She was going to Kōhunga Reo and we would have argued that cause. We parted, pleased with the meeting.

I reach the street connecting the bottom end of Matai St. Past Kay Davies's house, the retarded girl, who Old Mr Green purportedly *interfered with*. He gave her rides on his horse and sledge, when he went up the hill to cut the mānuka firewood. Past John Henry's house. Many a rugby game I won against him on that back lawn. I came around the corner at the bottom of the hill and remember David Sutherland and Keith Murdock, sitting again in chairs at the top of the hill, threatening not to let us young kids home from school. I was only five and bawled my eyes out, desperate to get past. Today I continue past Sutherlands' place and up to the section where our house had stood. I look fairly cursively from the bottom so as not to attract local attention. I move on around the corner and take the top road at the bottom of the bush line. I make for the bush, always my refuge from the violence of school, the trips to town, having to dress up and do the social puppet dance. Today I find a good place in the sun, giving me a private vantage point of the whole area. I smoke, and drink coffee from the thermos flask.

Terry was the eldest, my father's son to his first wife. She had died of consumption. Terry was wild and reckless, subject to violent outbursts of anger. He bore the physical burden of work and the problems at home. He was about four years older than me and always fought to protect his younger brothers and sisters. Rebellious at school, he was put in the special class. He was good to me, even though the exploits he took me on sometimes frightened the shit out of me.

When Terry was thirteen, he and a couple of mates started putting bits of wood under the wheels of the school train. They got bigger and bigger, until they derailed three carriages with a sleeper. Terry took to his scrapers up the hill as fast as his legs could go. He waited for some of the shocked school pupils as they staggered forth and asked them what had happened to the train. One kid, it was reported, ran all the way home to St Leonards, in a shocked state. Terry got six months probation and took all the rap, refusing to name his mates.

I look at where the house had stood. I introvert deeply to where it still stands in a distant corner of my mind. Pain and joy run in poignant streams from those ravaged walls. The neighbours eventually carried the boards away, to keep warm, as it lay desolate. I visualise overgrown paths where I rode my flash new bike with gears. While careering down one day, the sheep's tethering rope was stretched taut across the path, about waist height. I hit that rope at downhill speed and flipped the bike in a somersault, landing winded, but seriously unhurt, on my back, gasping like a wounded mouse.

I sit again in the warm kitchen with its open fire, listening to the Archers on the radio with my mum after school. I ran all the way up the hill from the bus stop, to be home first and share that time. We drank tea and talked. In the fifties the Empire smiled benevolently, solid. Mum dreamed of home and the printing factory, back in Manchester. Biking out in the country on sunny Sunday afternoons with her friends. A good, sensible girl, with a bloom in her cheeks and a song in her heart. Jet black hair and laughing blue eyes. She was small but brave. Try and pull one over my Mum, Mr rip-off shopkeeper. She stood up to anyone, no matter how big.

I feel the acrid smell of the fertiliser smoke and confront the pain. My father's drunken anger, staggering up the path. The slam of the chairs in the kitchen,

"Where's my bloody tea!"

Bolt upright in bed now all the kids listening. Hoping she won't say anything.

"You're nothing but a bastard!"

A rising crescendo of fear. Fighting off emotional panic. I get up and try to calm Roseanne and Jim who are crying in the passageway beside the kitchen door. I know that their emotional control is less than mine. I force myself to remain calm. Panic is the fruit of fear. He slaps her across the mouth with an open hand and she falls against the biscuit tin on the shelf, cutting her head. She abuses him, calling him all the bastards under the sun. He grumbles but thankfully restrains. On other nights Terry forced himself between them in an effort to protect her. We knew that her safety was the key to our salvation. The kids come in and clutch our mother, who cries and shouts, slowly calming down. Good warm sleep was always appreciated in that house.

Mother of God pray for us
Mother of the perpetual succour, succour us.

The harbour is blue gem stone in the sunlight. Tuis and Kererū are plentiful here. Across the other side I see the brick exterior of Waverly convent. We did a couple of lags there. When Martin was born, I was seven or eight, and all us kids spent a couple of weeks inside, over the confinement period.
      They alienated family groupings and split us up over various age and sex categories. I ended up in a dormitory of boys. Military style single bed spacings. A boy who was later in my class at Christian Brothers slept in the bed next to mine. Each morning I was awakened by his cries for mercy. Several early morning nuns dragged him from his cold, piss soaked bed where he lay shivering. They pulled his arms roughly and tore his piss smelling pyjamas from his bare, red arse. He screamed and wailed, fearful cries of shame, hoping for mercy. They strapped his bare arse with their straps, tattooing red welts while he screamed and wriggled. That inflamed the anger and they strapped him with greater justification. They punched, thumped and stood over him, telling him what a filthy, dirty wretch he was. He scurried, stumbling before the crucifix worn on their belts, powerless, exposed and shamed, remaking his bed to atone for his abject filthiness. God forbid that any future man could torment such a one as he lies rotting in some park next to his sherry bottle. Only great love can cure such pain.

Hail Mary pray for us
Mea culpa, mea culpa, mea maxima culpa

Each week we had to line up and change the hand me down clothes. After the first week I was verbally abused for having biscuit crumbs caught in my wool jersey. I felt the shame. One time to impress Terry, I got into trouble for spitting down the stairs on other boys. I received a good strapping, which I had learned to take without flinching, holding my suffering within. Towards the end Terry broke out with some older boys, and they didn't find them until after dark.

Roseanne, Jimmy and I, were the favourite act, at the Saturday night concerts. We sang:

I'm a rambler I'm a gambler, a long way from home.
Or
There was a wild colonial boy, Jack Duggan was his name.
Or
Bold Robert Emmet, the darling of Ireland
Bold Robert Emmet will die with a smile.

But the grand finale that always brought the house down was;

Two little orphans a boy and a girl, sat by the old church door.

Each evening we were assigned chores, but I always made my way down to the warmth of the kitchen. There was a loving, warm natured nun in that kitchen who liked me. I worked well for her.
 The tui song is drowned by the rooster. A dog voices its sullen anger on this Ravensbourne afternoon. I sit among the winter, dead head grasses that sprinkle sunlight. The bare sycamores stir new life. I watch a distant dog point its tail at me and shit. Ravensbourne: haphazard back yards, motley collection of sheds, hutches, kennels, sheep pens, and random gardens. A flash of pink. A young girl, could be Roseanne, walks down the road towards the harbour in black tight slacks and pink top, alternating shadow and brilliant sun flashes. Yes, you are silent O Tui. Wonder in awe at this beautiful flower of female delight. I nestle into the enfolding softness of sun drenched, long grass. The earth is tender, smelling of pollen.
 I remember those Dunedin backyards. At age eleven I attended the Christian Brothers boxing classes on Friday night with my mate Dennis. Dennis was big, brash and brave, wildly imaginative. On dark Friday nights we used to walk from the school to the railway station without using the streets, travelling over fences and through backyards. Behind those dark brick facades we entered a world of steep, sloping sections with tack-on buildings in profusion. Pieces of old fence and discarded lattices lay covered in nasturtium, biddy bids and pumpkin vines. Tall, black trees stood sentinel, silhouetting moon-swept chimney pots. Rubbish tins clattered, dogs barked, men swore and we scurried.
 We scrambled out of the backyards somewhere down the bottom of Rattray St, hurrying through the Exchange before crossing into Queens Gardens. Dunedin houses are a mixture of imperial red brick, stone and timber. That Exchange was once the grand business centre. Roman columns in Oamaru stone symbolise classical grandeur. They have not turned their backs on the past in Dunedin. Even the whore-house today is dressed in the decadent facade of Roman Empire.

I fought some battles in those Ravensbourne backyards. Coming home from school one afternoon, in my eleventh year, I passed Sutherland's gate and heard cries for help coming from my brother Martin who was locked in the chook house. He was only five and I saw John Sutherland, who was thirteen, patrolling the enclosure with a willow stick. My first instinct was to keep walking but shame stopped me. I turned back and went down to the chook house.
"Let him out Sutherland!"
I reached for the chook house latch and Sutherland whacked me across the knuckles with the willow stick. I turned to face him and before I knew what was happening he had me backed up against a tree with one hand around my throat, threatening to smash me with the crowbar that he had raised with the other. With all the strength I could muster I smacked him full in the face with a right. He staggered back, and then advanced kicking and swearing, enraged. I grabbed his boot lifting it high and kicked his back leg from under him. I drove him point blank on his arse into the ground. He came at me again for the same result. This time he lay winded and blubbering, staying down. I unlocked the chook house and took Martin home.

They were a tough family those Sutherlands. I saw the oldest brother Jerry at sixteen ride his motor bike down the street provocatively towards his old man. Old Barry stood grizzled, in the middle of the street with a large lump of wood in his hands. Jerry roared up close, as if to run him down, only to skid and turn back a number of times. Old Barry cursed him, standing tall, hoping for the chance to smash him right off his bike. Coming out the gate another day, I saw John running past me with fear and panic on his face. His brother Cyril chased him with a knife. Every few steps Cyril threw the knife at his back and then stooped to re-gather it on the run.

Cyril was a real warrior and I always admired him. Even though he was older we became good friends and he used to let me smoke the cigarettes, hidden in the chook house, that he stole from town. I met him some years ago and we talked together over a pint. He was always getting into fights. He told me that when he was younger he sometimes hired himself out as a standover man for drug dealers. It was his job to collect outstanding monies. He paid a visit to a big Canadian who was staying in a flat with plenty of mates for support and asked the bloke to pay. Cyril told him that he would be back on Tuesday and he expected the money. The bloke felt pretty secure and told him to piss off. Cyril withdrew and wondered what he could do to get his attention. On the appointed day he knocked on the door and demanded the cash. The bloke told him to piss off again, so Cyril took out a can of lighter fluid and drenched the bastard. He whipped out a zippo lighter and holding it up to the bloke's face asked for the money again. This time he got paid.

A train grumbles and whistles in the distance. A day earlier Margaret and I had travelled in my old school train out towards the Taieri Gorge. We caught it from the Dunedin Railway Station, which today lives awkwardly in semi-retirement. Margaret in long black coat, funky hat and scarf, hurries across the railway station to the ladies. I gaze at the tile work and the Victorian colonnades. Several wedding couples pose for photos with their entourages, basking in the decaying remnants of imperial grandeur. Japanese tourists photograph the wedding couples while they are being photographed. Freezing this moment in time and capturing their illusion of grandeur for as long as paper lasts. Cross-cultural facades are somehow more imposing. In such a grand world as this it was hard to imagine that they had toilets. That somewhere in a back room beneath the veil you would eventually discover a world of curlers, makeup, bed socks, hidden rolls of fat, tissues and tantrums, periods and sanitary pads.

Never mind that this old school train goes the wrong way. We find a deserted carriage at the front and sit luxuriant in wood panelled splendour. I see the shopping bag, net, luggage racks. The well built toilet cubicles and entry ways. This train was once captive to the random madness of boys, segregated by schools to various carriages. The train begins to move and speak its own story.

Clickety clack, you Catholic rat.
Rumble and creak, you protestant freak.
Punch the guard and steal his hat
The bastards got pimples, his arse is fat

Clickety clack, I'll punch you, you rat
Clickety,clickety clickety clack.

Rush of wind through vacuum tunnel.

Now that you've left
You can never go back,
Clickety clack
never go back.
Watch the wind,
clickety clack
Grab your hat
Now's where you're at.

Margaret with eyes shining on the outside balcony, sunlit wind in her hair, flashes of gold, Celtic earrings. We gaze on the industry of the Taieri Plains, fertile farms growing good food. Even I have to admit it's better now than when it was a flax swamp. Perhaps the civilising influence of immigration has some good side. The plough was not pulled in vain here. We flow on through the gentle beauty of willow graced river banks, until we reach the awesome majesty of the Gorge. Natural rock hewn cathedrals among which Arawata Bill foraged for gold. Was a God to be found here also, among this distant Sinai?

    I stop scribbling and take out my anthology of NZ poets. I cannot see the land as those early poets did. They painted man's alienation from nature, caught up in the finger nail struggle to survive under the eye of a capricious God who ministered justice through violent storms and flash floods. When we spent those years in the bush up North, hunting for the pot and living without electricity, we perceived a different spirit. An awesome beauty that released a better nature within. The secret is to flow with, not fight. Let yourself be absorbed into its pulse. The real threat is man's materialistic desire to dominate, manipulating the spirit for personal gain. As a result concrete and tar choke the breathing tubes of the earth mother. Her arteries have become sewers flowing with the excrement of men.

    On a cold, wet Sunday morning we climb Rattray St, past Speight's Brewery to St Joseph's Cathedral. A grafted echo of medieval Europe's religio–political grandeur, when powerful rulers invoked a rule-bound God to hold the ignorant masses in bondage. Classical colonnades and marble altar signify rigid power hewn from stone. Stained glass windows glisten as jewels depicting the obedience of the saints. St Patrick, John, Margaret, Bridget, Cornelius, Celestine. The colourful pantheon of the Knights of the Holy Roman Catholic Empire blended in a pagan-christian syncretism. Children from the local school had hung a sheet of cartridge paper on the pillars which said that St Bridget was kind, loving, compassionate, stood up for herself and believed in God. I thought of my own daughter with satisfaction. We knelt in the awkward wooden pews. The place was quite full. Arched wooden confessionals still set into the stone walls.

Bless me Father for I have sinned. It is three weeks since my last confession. Since then I have had: bad thoughts and actions, swore at my brother, and not done what my parents told me........

I see again the Stations of the Cross captured in the statuesque plaster pictures upon which I had gazed in reverent wonder. What did this event have to do with me? This poignant suffering of desperate love. A lurid example of the cruelty of man? We felt the thirty nine lashes and stumbled under the cross. I sympathised with the cross but hoped to avoid carrying one. We'll get ya you bastard, no matter how big you think you are. Jesus I'm sorry for what they did to you. Jesus I suffer also in silent pain. Mary offered a smiling mother love, nurturing softer feelings.

Hail Mary, full of grace.
The Lord is with you.

With that mystic spell I faced the violent barbs. My family seemed the incarnation of both God's love and his suffering. Confession released us for a while to gambol in relieved joy. But alas, the return of that acrid cloud, heralding another belt of pain and weeping.

Jesus, look how you still loved Peter.
Dare I think you could love me?
I am the mixed blessing that I am.
Alternating weak and strong.
Like him I pulse powerful flashes of invincibility,
hounded by the dogs of guilt and fear.

Kim Barr must have come from a seriously dysfunctional home. He had sat in these pews with my class at school, a tall, lonely boy. There were 68 pupils in that class. One time he went missing and the story flashed around that he had run away. He was found by the police three days later sleeping out in the Octagon and returned to school. The morning he came back there was a subdued hush in the class. The teaching brother was mid-thirties, fair and handsome, cruel and heartless. He laboured hard at ramming information down the throat of the thick heads, with a vigorous range of punishment techniques. He whacked our knuckles with the edge of the ruler. He grabbed the short hair round our temples and shook us, threw chalk and dusters and pretty much had free rein to work out the frustrations inherent in his life of celibate monasticism. He educated us with the alacrity of an SS agent.

    He made Kim Barr wait until just after the Angelus time. A deathly hush fell over the class as he called him out. There was some verbal bullying to warm up and then he ordered Kim Barr to the room off the entry. He made him strip to his undies and bend over. He took out his leather strap. About an inch thick and 16 inches long. Kim Barr bends over, whimpering. He takes a warm up swing across the lower buttocks slightly below the edge of the undie line. Kim Barr screamed, we listened. He screamed his way through six lashes with the brother holding him down, vigorous with rage. Kim Barr had his cross to carry.

A year later I jumped on his cross, making it heavier. I picked a fight with him in the playground. It rapidly turned into a full on donnybrook with a large circle of the school gathered. He was a head taller than me and tough. I moved forward, boring up with a steady stream of punches to try and get under his guard and smash his face in, while he moved back, fighting me off with a longer reach. When it was finally broken up I knew it had been touch and go. Me and Kim Barr ended up weeding the brother's garden for the rest of lunchtime and got on quite well. I took the advice of my dad after that.

Never pick a fight Paddy, but never run away from one.

On Saturday evening, as was my custom, I went to the play at the local pub. It was on the south side of the city, old and homely, no students here. On offer was a performance more modern than Pinter and as exuberant as a Brechtian troupe. The locals were fair pumping, as they had been drinking all afternoon, waiting for the league game. The sound system piped out vintage nostalgia, as I took my pint to a stool in the corner. Front row seats, yet unobtrusive. About twenty patrons shambled around tables near the bar on the other side of the pool table.

The hit man was tall and raw boned. Tough looking with long, balding hair. He was pissed mellow, with all his attention on the woman beside him. She was mid-thirties, still with a good figure. Meanly attractive face, with freckles and a tight lipped, bitter edge, indicating that life had been tough. She was drunk, inviting him to fondle her. Snuggling in, she rubs herself seductively over him, enjoying this moment of power. They kiss full on and paw one another in between drinks.

The chief protagonist stood on the other side of the table. He was also large, with a bald head and looked as though he still worked out. He was next to a whore from the escort parlour. She was young, pierced and ripely plump, sitting on the bar stool so that her slit skirt displayed black stockings up to her fat buttocks.

The Jester cavorted on my side of the tables. He was late forties with half his teeth missing, an inoffensive funny guy who threatened no one. No wonder he could afford to laugh among such random chaos. He staggered about the pool table, cracking jokes and laughing loudly at his own. When a good rock number ripped out of the stereo, which was being manipulated full volume by hit man to make a point, Jester grabs the pool cue and begins to strut his stuff. He was top shit. He performed with balls and passion, very good dance routines and his miming of the songs was excellent. Oh! Blighted talent to die here. If only he could have got out of vaudeville and tried some serious acting. Like playing a life. That sensitive, creative streak within him was not nurtured in this Dunedin school of working class hard knocks.

Hit man's drunken slut began an argument with the protagonist over a misunderstanding with a dish cloth. He told her off, quite rightly and firmly. The slut began to whine, but hit man slobbered reassurance, grabbing her to him, telling the protagonist to fuck off. Face was saved. It was just a display of aggression and both the boys had realised some time ago that at their age it was easier to reduce it to rituals. The slut from the whore house purred her way through, unperturbed, sipping her beer. I realised she was stoned. The sound system fair pumped out a raging orchestral, Spanish, jazz fandango. The bar rocked, shouted, laughed, let go, contently inebriated from the daily pain. I took an intermission and bought another pint before returning to my seat.

The jester got comical during his pool game. Next to him sat a fat, blonde women in her forties. She was a friendly cow. I was pleased to see Jester playing touchy touchy and giving her a bit of a giggle. She grabs his balls from behind just at the moment of impact on the break. He fair jumps into the shot. He puts his arm round her and gives her a bit of a cuddle. Isn't it grand I thought;

That everybody can find somebody to love.

Hit man and drunken slut staggered off to unzip on the privacy of another set, while the survivors of the fandango settled down to watch the league. The patrons perched on bar stools with their backs to me, staring at the screen. The bar grew quiet. As the game picked up the patrons began grunting and wowing as the boys put in good hits. The play was over, with the actors seeking the obscurity of fantasy. I left the theatre and stepped out into the cold street.

They had begun pigeon perched, at the drama piece we had attended one university lunchtime. Margaret and I, hand in hand, enjoying glimpses of past student nostalgia. The players perched at the wise feet of the television screen looking lost and wayward. A deceitful spirit emerged and offered them: health, wealth or happiness. They considered each alternately. Health alone was seen as interminably boring. Wealth, a life of sleazy consumerism. Happiness was very poorly painted as though unimaginable. Who wants to limit the options? In the end they choose what they already had, which was why the deceitful spirit could grant the wish. Can we as easily grasp who we are and shed the cross? That sort of play wouldn't have gone big with the pub patrons I thought. Not enough balls. Shakespeare had the right idea, keep the ignorant entertained while leaving those who are able, to consider the greater things.

A pub jazz band played on our final night, when we took our daughter and friends out to dinner. The average age in the band was over seventy. They played the jazz standards of their world, still with vigour. The trumpet clear and youthful sang of the unfettered spirit within. The drummer was tight, still doing just enough, economically and with skill. They enjoyed their playing. They were doing what they liked. We were just settling in to enjoy them when my daughter discovered that her boyfriend had been rushed to hospital with the potential quick killer, meningitis.

And while the jazz band played
a young man stared into the doorway of shadows.
Where does that pathway of suffering lead?
Do we dance and cavort across a scripted stage
Or rebound impulsively amid life's random chaos?
Young man while you wait for the composer to do his thing
Pick up thy instrument and learn how to sing.

Saying It Like It Is

Early in the sixties Peter Sellers released a record of his comedy work. One track was a political speech by a Tory MP that goes on for many tedious minutes and says absolutely nothing. Retrospectively I realise that it represents a fairly accurate picture of reality, but then I considered it brilliant satire. It gripped my creative soul, presenting me a pre-Pinteresque glimpse of the theatre of the absurd. I wondered if I could do that.

One Friday night I was drinking in the Fitzherbert with some teaching mates. I retold, for their amusement, snippets from Seller's speech. Somehow the telling simply wasn't enough.

"I bet you I could go up to Broadway now and give a speech like that," I commented. The bets were made and while most of them drifted off to other appointments I made my way up into the Square accompanied by Phil, who had been selected as the official observer. It was about 7pm when we reached the ANZ steps just opposite the traffic lights on the corner of the Square and Broadway. Friday shoppers and movie-goers thronged the street and the traffic was busy. I took my stance and amid all the street noise began . . .

"Brothers and sisters I appeal to you tonight, because there are many problems, at the present time, that need to be considered with heartfelt concern by all of us right minded citizens. This is not the time to bury one's head in the sand, as if these challenges were of no consequence. This is surely the time, for those of us who have a conscience, and are prepared to meet the challenge, to take a step forward in the unity that binds us as a nation. We must make sacrifices now to put in place the structural concepts that I am convinced hold the answers to our deepest problems . . ."

A group of people attracted by the unusual sight of a street orator stopped and listened. Obviously being drawn to the wisdom of my words, they stayed. Much encouraged I redoubled my efforts.

"It is indeed unnecessary to remind you that nationhood has never been forged by the diplomatic folly of disunity. No, a nation is forged when people take back the prevailing history of the past and remake it in a way that holds relevance to our future. Brothers and sisters don't be fooled by the mindless politics of the current ethos. Does not this great country of ours belong to those of us who must arise, in flight from the grass roots of mediocrity, in order to set the present house in order. . .?"

The crowd swelled rapidly. People pushed forward at the back to listen to this fine political oratory. I emphasised the most pungent points with extravagant gestures and the sincerity dripped off me to mingle with the sweat of genuine effort. I was as happy as a pig in shit.

After ten minutes the impact of my speech had brought the street almost to a standstill. The crowd spilled over the pavement onto the roadway and blocked half the street. The traffic lights controlling the busiest intersection on Broadway were rendered dysfunctional because the cars were now unable to negotiate the pedestrian crossing. Most satisfying artistically, I noted that nobody was leaving. They hung onto every word I flung down, as though at last they had met a leader who told it like it was. A gang of bikies arrived adding to the noise and mayhem. They revved their engines and parked them provocatively across the now pedestrian roadway. At last art had triumphed over technology. With only one short speech I had won back this small part of the kingdom. For a brief moment the whimsical urges of the human spirit had broken free from the mathematically dominated dogtrot. For a brief moment spontaneous mayhem ruled, if only because it felt good.

But alas, just like the Irish Easter rebellion of 1916 the greatest victories can be short lived. Halfway through mid sentence I turned to see two police constables standing beside me.

"All right mate you've had your fun, now bugger off."
"And what will you do if I refuse," I answered cockily, fired up by the revolutionary power of my own speech.
"We'll arrest you and put you in the cells for the night."

It is an attested historical fact that some of the greatest political careers have been the shortest ones. Take Norm Kirk for example. I also hasten to add that at this stage Nelson Mandela was still locked up and I had recently watched a film in which Ghandi was slowly kicked unconscious as he knelt before a railway track. More importantly, I had already exceeded the parameters of the bet. Finally, however, I must confess that, due to a prevailing weakness of character, I would rather attend a good party than gaze upon a rampant moon through rectangular bars. All these factors combined to help me see the practical wisdom of the constable's words. I decided to quit political leadership, at least for the time being.

"Fair enough mate," I said,"'we'll leave you to it then."
With a final wave to the crowd, I nodded to Phil and we walked across the street and into the gardens on the corner of the Square. Flushed with success I was about ready to find the nearest pub, however my recent converts would have none of it. This carnival had developed a momentum of its own. By the time we reached the gardens I was surrounded by a large

group of bikies and assorted riff raff who had firmly decided that they would follow me to hell and back. At last, a leader who could liberate that stifled part of them. Something was finally happening.

Feeling rather flattered by the prominence into which I had been thrust, and not one to leave before the fat lady sang, I mounted the steps of the wishing well and opened up again on a more Marxist stance.

"What this country needs is not the parsimonious disquiet of red faced old men, who belch and fart trite platitudes about security and saving for the future. What this country needs is men and women of courage who have the vision to rise up and grasp the ripened tit of fate. To suck the very nectar of destiny. The technological shackles of injustice must be flung aside in the search for honest expressions of moral pugilism. We must rise together and join forces in an articulate brotherhood which will have the power to redefine the lost meaning of altruism."

These words introduced a decidedly revolutionary fervour. Many of the disciples were now swigging from opened beer bottles and in an undoubted attempt to throw some light on the subject; someone had started a fire in the park rubbish tin.

It is another amazing truism of history that great movements seldom begin in isolation. Rather, social upheaval begins like a summer rain. Individual drops congeal together to produce a number of disparate rivulets which eventually form a larger river to sweep away all opposition in its march to the freedom of the ocean. Such was the case at this climactic moment.

My friend Api suddenly materialised at my shoulder.

"Hey Pad, give me a hand with Mart will you!"
"Mart, why, what's the matter?"
"The cops are chasing him," he answered.
"There he is!"

We looked and beheld my brother Martin stripped to the waist, riding a stolen bicycle through the shrubbery with a child's plastic policeman's hat on his head. He was closely followed by the two constables who chased him vigorously but were unfortunately no match for the stolen bicycle. Mart laughing and gesticulating changed direction every now and again just to make an even contest of it. The cops looked angry. Whereas they could forgive the bicycle, that plastic policeman's hat was an insult not to be borne. Again they gave pursuit as Martin turned and headed in the opposite direction. Being a writer, Api gave chase in an attempt to save them all from themselves, but feeling the responsibility of a much greater calling I refrained from entering the game.

Taking the opportunity offered by the constable's preoccupation I spoke again. By now, though, my words were becoming tempered by a growing pattern of lawlessness among the brotherhood. The bikies were ready for a scrap. They had taken my words to heart, a fire to ignite the belly of their rebellious spirit. Mart appeared again around the side of the wishing well, pedalling like hell with the policeman's hat still firmly in place. No sign of the cops. I took it that he had temporarily shattered their morale. Taking a cue from this timely demonstration of heroic flight, I left the steps and melted into the shrubbery.

"Hey Phil," I called. "Its dry bloody work being a politician, let's bugger off back to the pub."
And quietly leaving the Friday night chaos, frothing with its meaningless bubbles of fragmentary hope we crept, like the phoenix, back to cheerful obscurity.

Helping the Boss Out

One late night she blew in across a drizzled car park. Jean Sloane, the town bike. Shivering inside her black stockings and short imitation leather skirt. She had shoulder length hair, greasy and unkempt, framing a hawkish face that sprouted a few pimples, thinly disguised by heavy make up. A bit thick, she sometimes ordered coffee and hung around wanting to chat. This morning was the worst time to pick. Two a.m. after trade had fallen off was when they usually got a bit of sleep. He had been just about to take a nap on the easy chair in the boss's office, while his brother Jim made himself comfortable on the potato sacks out in the back kitchen. Jean slid open the front door of the restaurant and called out for coffee.

Annoyed and desperate for sleep, he staggered out to the front counter and served her. She unbuttoned her leopard skin vinyl coat and made herself comfortable, warming her hands around the cup.

"Have you been busy?"
"No, pretty quiet actually. We're more or less closed you know. We use this time to prepare the vegies for the next day." His attempt at subtlety was wasted.
"I saw your boss George up town the other day. He said hello to me."
"Bet he said goodbye to you too," mimicked Jim, from the back kitchen, who was still half pissed from the evening session at the pub. George was the short, portly, middle aged, balding man, who owned and managed the restaurant. They all worked seven days a week over the summer and sometimes as many as eighteen hours a day. They did the night shift and George who worked days had only recently bundled up a pile of papers and headed off to his bed, exhausted.

A sly demon entered him. Maybe it was dwelling in that half conscious world of sleep deprivation, or perhaps the adrenaline rush of desperation, but at least it gave him the motivation to stay awake.

"George likes you."
"What do you mean, George likes me?"
"He told me. Just the other day he was saying to me. I like that Jean Sloane."
"Oh yeah, pull the other tit," she sniggered over her coffee, relaxing a bit and enjoying the sudden attention.
"Well I'm just telling you what he told me, and anyway I thought you'd like to know. I mean, it seems a shame that compatible people don't get together just because they're too shy to let each other know."

She sat up at this and crossed her leg, letting a bit of thigh show, and pulled out her lipstick bag with an intrigued, half-smile.
"What did he say about liking me?"
"Look I shouldn't really say anything. Now don't you tell him I told you, but he said that he thought you were a kind, thoughtful person."
Jim's guffaws erupted from the back kitchen while his own sides shook all over the bar stool.
"Is that all he said?" She sounded a bit disappointed that he might be having her on.

Pulling himself together he rallied again.
"I think he fancies you."
"Oh he fancies me does he, what gave you that big idea?"
"Cause I've seen him looking at you when you come in."
"Aw bullshit!" She stubbed her cigarette in the ashtray, fighting back.

He got off his stool and spent a bit of time tidying up around the milkshake makers and poured them both another cup of coffee. He needed time to think.
"Tell her to get out of here," said Jim who was stretched out across the potato sacks. "I'm bloody knackered."
"You watch," he boasted. "I bet I can get her to ring George."

"Lots of marriages seem to be breaking up these days," he ventured casually, regaining his seat behind the counter. She half shrugged. "Well, I seem to be blamed for enough of them," darting a raised eyebrow to investigate the effect.
"No, I mean, today it even seems to happen to people you don't expect."
"Why, who have you been hearing about?"
"Someone you know."
"Who?"
"Well." He carried on wiping the bench. She put down her cup, impatiently fixing him with a look of exasperation.
"Someone we talked about before," he said quietly, picking up the broom and walking out the back.

"Here, have some of this," said Jim, handing him the last bottle they had been saving to ease the splitting head and dry mouth.
"Tell her to piss off! I want some bloody sleep."
"Who were you talking about?" she demanded loudly through the servery.
"The one we talked about before. George."
"Is George's marriage breaking up?"

"Bloody quick on the uptake isn't she," sniggered Jim. "I wish she was half as bloody quick at pissing off, my bed will have turned to french fries before I get to sleep."

Composing himself he went out the front and refilled her cup.
"Yeah, look don't tell anyone I told you, will you. Not many people know about it. Apparently George's wife is a bit frigid and she doesn't meet his needs as a man much. Well, he's finally had to look elsewhere to get a bit, so to speak."
"Gee!" she exclaimed, genuinely overwhelmed by the quality of the night's gossip.
"Yeah, so he's been having a bit of a hard time lately, I suppose that's how come he noticed you."
"Oh bullshit! he noticed me," she cackled.

"Yeah well fair enough, I shouldn't have told you. It'll only get me into trouble with the boss. Forget I said anything."
"Aw come on," she pleaded, tapping a fag vigorously on the packet. "I won't tell him you told me. When did he notice me?"
"Well it was nothing really. Last week I noticed he was standing in the servery looking through the hatch. He seemed to be there for a long time so I looked to see what he was looking at." He paused to tidy the confectionery stand.
"What was he looking at?"
"At you."
"Aw crap!" she cackled.
"No, look fair go, you were sitting just like you are now and we could see up your skirt. George was having an eye full. All right Boss?" I said.
 "Bloody oath," he reckoned. "That Jean Sloane is all right. Look at those legs. That's class. I bet she gets the rich fellas with plenty of money and flash cars."
"What else did he say?" She pulled at her too short skirt and swivelled to reveal laddered black stockings running up to thin white thighs.
"No, he didn't say anything else. Not that time."
"Well, what did he say the other time," she demanded.
"Look, you'd better not say anything to George. You'll get me in the shit. I was talking to him the other day about his marriage bust up and he just happened to say he couldn't wait to be out of all the domestic crap so that he could concentrate on getting a classy sheila like Jean Sloane."

He wiped the counter busily while she lit her fag. She considered deeply and then looking at him, somewhat bitterly exclaimed.

"Bullshit! I'll tell you why it's bullshit, because if he's that keen how come he hasn't said anything?"
"Well!" he replied indignantly. "It just shows you don't know him as well as I do."
"I've known him longer," she retorted protectively.
"Yeah, but he doesn't confide in you like he does with me. See, you wouldn't know it but George is very shy."

"He's not shy when it comes to making us shout at the bloody boozer," contributed Jim.
"Shut up you mongrel. No I wasn't talking to you. It's ok. I was just giving instructions to my brother. Look why don't you just give him a ring sometime, it's easier to talk over the phone."
"What would I want to ring him for?" she mocked.
"Well just to encourage him not to be too shy to make an approach. Tell him that you find him quite attractive."
"Aw, I couldn't do that."
'Why not? Look I think it's a damn shame when two attractive people miss out on getting together just because they are both too shy to make contact. Surely that's worth making some effort for? We can't leave it all to the bloody stars. That's why there's so many lonely people out there. If I was you, I'd be on the phone tonight and get it sorted out."

"I can't ring him now anyway, he'll be asleep."
"No he won't, he just left before you came in and he always has a bit of a read before he goes to sleep. You'll get him now if you ring. Look here's the number." He laid the piece of card beside her cup.
"Oh you're just talking a load of crap!"

"Look!" he declared hotly. "It won't make any difference to me whether you ring him or not. I'm just thinking of you two. Just trying to do the decent thing and help out. Look what thanks I get for my trouble! If you don't bloody well ring, then I know he'll be too shy to say anything, and he'll end up with someone else. There's plenty of women out there today who wouldn't think twice about ringing the man they wanted. If you want to grow into an old spinster then that's your look out. If I was you I'd make a move while I was still young and attractive."

She seemed to like that last bit. She sat up straight on the stool studying her profile in the servery mirror.
"Where's the phone?"
He passed the phone across the counter, struggling to appear disinterested. He walked out the back again but observed her unseen through the servery

hatch. Jim was off the potato sacks peering around the other side. They couldn't believe he had nearly pulled it off. The sheer bloody cheek. The awesome power of manipulating her to a pre-determined course of action. And of course the perfect kick up the arse for the boss!

George was a bit on the greasy side himself. It was true that he was not getting enough at home. He wanted to party, but his wife was boring and straight. George, as a successful small businessman, with the luxury of a till to help him out, was more than happy to chase a piece of skirt, except he wasn't very good at it. He operated on the level of smutty jokes, Playboy Magazines and he regularly embarrassed the young waitresses with inappropriate gropings. They knew they had a beauty on him this time. If only she would ring.

"Hello. Is that you, George?"
The madness of the moment annihilated them. They laughed until they could hardly draw breath, staggering about while trying desperately to listen. How persistent she was. I mean, it wouldn't have been easy to cope with George. Woken up in the middle of the night with a call from the town's most notorious skirt and having to talk on the bed phone while lying next to his bitchy wife. Explain that. It became obvious that Jean was a little non-plussed with the reception but they admired the way she seemed able to hang in there. She damn well said her piece and there was no easy getting rid of her.
When they finally heard her say,
"Well, look, don't be shy; if you fancy me I think you might as well be honest and just say so,"
they collapsed in pulsating orgasms of overwhelming hilarity. The tears streamed down their faces.

Jean left not long after the phone call. She seemed a bit subdued and more than a little preoccupied. She just walked out like she did most nights. Pulling her coat around her scrawny neck she blew back out into the swamp wind.

First light brought a few early breakfasts with the two of them awake and on top of the job. They both got a couple of hours sleep after Jean left and knew that shortly, when the day-girls got in, they had finished their 14 hour shift. They suspected, too, that George would be in pretty early that morning and sure enough right on cue he entered.

They sniggered in anticipation as his car pulled up sharply in the drive. They could tell that he meant business the way he leapt straight out and slammed the car door. He strode determinedly across the car park. He looked bloody furious as he grasped the handle and swung open the door. The moment he stepped in he was struck in the middle of his bald head with a large jumbo container full of water that Jim had balanced above on an ice cream stick. The water drenched his face and the front of his shirt. They laughed at him. The sort of laughter that screamed, hey boss, you don't own us. We only work here because we choose to.

His startled look melted as he stood with the water dripping off his face. He just looked stupid and utterly speechless. They laughed louder. Without a word he turned and escaped into his office with the derision still ringing in his ears. An hour later, just as they were finishing the breakfast shift, he emerged playing his bustling, efficient self, just as if nothing had happened.

They worked there that next summer too and not one word regarding that incident was ever mentioned between them.

The Poetry Reading

Then there was the time that me and Tiki took the acid in Wellington. He was trying to do the respectable bit at the time. He had managed to slide out of University, but influenced by his father he accepted a course at Journalism School. They were rather middle class and lacked a sense of humour at the Journalism school. Far too earnest to appreciate Tiki's persistent range of troublesome difficulties. They were also very strict on absenteeism. To gain sympathy Tiki played his back-block Māori boy routine. One of the lecturers, who was of liberal persuasion, took him under his wing and tried to nurse his undoubted talent through the ravages of culture shock. It was to this person that I found myself engaged in serious conversation, from the phone booth in the foyer of the journalism school, just as the acid started to bite. The faces of two Asian students leered idiotically in at me over the half booth wall.

Hello, its Constable Reece here from Central Metropolitan. I need to speak to Mr Tiki Hohepa. Yes I realise it's an inconvenience to take him out of class but we wish to deal with things as unobtrusively as possible. Look, if I could meet Mr Hohepa in the foyer then we could take the time to sort the matter out. He took the bait. Tiki appeared ten minutes later with a grin and a peculiar floating motion as he descended the stairs.

We made immediately for the nearest public bar and proceeded to down a few pints. Challenging for the pool table we settled in. Tiki told me that that night he had been asked to read some of his poems at Carmen's nightclub. He said that they were making a TV documentary on contemporary concerns and that they wanted people to read. You might as well come along and read too he said. I'll make sure that they put you on the programme.

I can't remember how we got out of the pubs late that afternoon. I have vague memories of Tiki being chased out by some big aggressive bastard. It was an advantage to be with Tiki on such occasions as they usually went for him, even though we both looked rough. I wore an old black overcoat and had shoulder length hair with a shark's tooth in my ear. Tiki looked like a scruffy Māori from the building site but after all I'm white and can talk with a middle class, educated accent in times of trouble. Alcohol put us in the mood to party, not to fight. Our mood at such times was cheeky with a leaning towards the macabre. We spent our time singing, telling stories and laughing at the random madness of life. Aggressive bastards sometimes didn't get the joke.

Somehow we emerged through that afternoon drunk, and negotiated our way to Carmen's for the night session. A lot of activity was happening in the relatively small confines of the nightclub. TV guys had set up several banks of cameras and light units. People stood on chairs and got things prepared for the performance. Tiki and I slipped out the back alley to smoke a joint. The walls gyrated vivid rust and assorted rubbish tins spilled their refuse about. Drizzle-splashed wind spat patterns on ragged drainpipes. Our attention was caught by a dandelion's defiant display of beauty as it gripped life through the narrow opportunity afforded by a concrete crack. We discussed moving it to a better place but wisely decided that a change of environment might alter its personality. Without the struggle it might not bloom.

Back inside, a local group of young Māori radicals had gathered. Middle class city Māori, who debated issues and had been given good profiles recently on documentary T.V. After an initial discussion Tiki launched into one of them. He told him he was just a wanker and would never be any use to anybody as long as his arse pointed to the ground. He threw in a rousing haka and then recited one of his protest poems for good measure. He had the attention of the bar now anyway. This was followed up with a derisive tirade about Māori politics. This is our land and it's you middle class pricks siting on the committees who're selling it. You better tell those foreign bastards to stop fishing any more of our kai moana. If you really cared about grass roots Māori you'd make sure the kai was left for us.

One of the radical group was about thirty, good looking with a fierce hurt look. Maybe he had a job as a social welfare officer during the day. He looked to me as though he didn't fit with working class Māori but had jumped on an intellectualised version of Māori protest rights, somewhere along the path as he completed a tertiary qualification. I imagined a neglected child, to a good-looking solo mother, who had been too busy to spend time with her son. To appease her guilt she had spoilt him. He sat looking sullenly handsome, oozing 'poor me'.

He was arguing with a woman of similar age. Short dark hair with attractive, part-Māori features. She looked butch, and well educated. They were sparring spiteful little university class jibes amid the clamour of Tiki and others. Suddenly the intensity became too much for him. He was losing ground completely and couldn't compete among the group. Not with Tiki in such dominant form for starters. To add to this, this fucking butch bitch, who reminded him of his mother, was beating him at sounding incisively intelligent. Suddenly he sprang up and gave her an angry, vicious whack on the side of the face. He punched his mother. Took the women back a peg or two I can tell you.

Amid this descent into chaos a nightclub bar was operating and an earnest, but worried TV producer was setting up a production. I caught glimpses of him peering concernedly over lighting poles positioned somewhat precariously around a raised stage area. At some point, a credit to his perseverance, he managed to get the show under way. With a whirl of television documentary filming, various people got up and read. Tiki was splendid and masterfully aggressive. His performance was given every ounce of passion as he blended traditional Māori chant with modern social reality.

At a suitable lull in the proceedings I decided it was my time to take the stage. I stood before the lights and began to read.

Thoughts in a Foxton Pub

Will I piss my life
Down the pungent urinal
Of a broken pub
While my friend's stroke my twisted balls?

Will my friend the publican
shed a tear
as he used to laugh
while I fed his family
and kept his wife in gin?

Who will fondle Rita Roberts bum
while she curses her husband
to delight the crowd
who, although feeling sorry for Tom
would rather feel his wife.

Who will listen to Allen,
stuttering spit into his beer,
recount with passion,
how he won the war
before lurching off
to beat his skinny wife

behind the bedroom door?

*Will they remember
I could hit three triple twenties,
hold my beer like a man,
always paid my way,
on pay day
anyway.*

*Or will my face
casually melt
among the froth clouds
of spittle-flecked laughter
sliding like coagulated phlegm
down the drain.*

This reading received a positive response from the gathered community so I prepared to proceed. As I was about to begin the earnest TV producer began pulling at my leg from the side of the stage. Who are you? he seemed to be saying. We are making a programme of modern Māori concerns. My themes are about the universally oppressed, I replied. I was a little annoyed at the interruption and felt that having been asked to bloody well read in this fucking mad house, then read I bloody well would. I returned to centre stage and started again.

Packaged Africa

*And here we have the perfect example
of the Omawaggawagga maiden.
Now firstly you will notice that the form
is very apelike,
almost, ah, human.
Although the hide is black
you will notice that it is quite sensitive to pain.
There! Notice the very inhuman cry
when I applied the match to the left udder.*

*The brain gentleman is as large as ours
But I am afraid
Through a lack of British imperialism
still functions in an apelike manner.
Notice also that no clothes are worn.*

*Now gentlemen
if you would like to move around
and poke it
feel free.
Don't be afraid gentlemen
the ropes are quite strong*

*Ah yes,
That Sir,
Seems to be the one thing
That is
quite human.*

An encouraging round of applause erupted from the establishment. The earnest TV prick persisted, however, and continued to harass me with lectures about his TV programme. You're not even Māori he said. Three cheers for your powers of observation you four eyed prick, I replied. Look, just fuck off mate, can't you see I'm bloody well coping with trying to perform here. I was enraged by the demonstrated injustices of the situation. These bastards were against me because I was white. I walked once more to the spot under the light and let the third poem slip deliberately to the floor.

*Listen!
My father is an Irishman
who was forced, by the ravages of British colonialism
to immigrate to NZ in 1946.
106 years after the treaty.*

*Neither him nor I
ever stole Māori land
or treated you with less respect
than you deserved.*

*Unfortunately today
it's us working class Pākehā
who are the real underprivileged
in this country.*

*I can't get my poems heard
because all the money
goes to
middle class Māori*

*who have your hands
firmly wrapped around the welfare
and literary grants.*

I left the stage giving the earnest TV prick a withering look. By now his programme had descended into the chaos he had feared. A glass was thrown amid the uproar, smashing spectacularly incandescent, as a stack of lights crashed to the floor. Fights and scuffles broke out across the room. People shouted and argued. I slipped quietly around the back of the stage to the bar and managed to get another drink.

Hours later we trudged up a hill overlooking Wellington city. Tiki and I at the end of a spree. Cold, wet, drizzled misery accompanied the bad end of a bender. We trudged quietly together knowing that nothing lasted forever. Not even misery.

Back at Tiki's flat I collapsed on a mattress on the floor with cold toes stuck halfway between the mattress and the couch. It was impossible to sleep with the head-grinding buzz of the speed in the acid. Outside it was now raining hard. An axe split my brain. Alcohol-washed visions of the night danced across the darkened room. Rolling over I staggered to my feet and got dressed. Sickness and nausea washed over me. Wrapped in my black wool overcoat I grabbed my pack and let myself out into the driving rain.

Walking to the edges of town I discovered it was about 5:30 a.m. It was still dark but the shops were lit, with owners bustling van loads of produce and stocking shelves. I bought a packet of cigarettes from a service station and huddled for a time out of the rain squalls under the porch. If that's the life of a poet they can stick it, I said to the rain. I gave up writing poetry after that.

St. George and a Dragon

I would tell the tale of heroes and dragons, the losers and losers of the electric tinsel age. I'll show you St George seated among a random spit of bodies that move as a beer froths. Smoke haze floats like stale mist seeking out bar lights and turning pastel among the band. But a style befitting the new heroic age. Chair angled three feet from the table, slightly tilted by long legs that spread defying a crowd. Pint grasped with a wide hand, strong, yet finely tuned by fret boards and pool cues. A body, large framed. Six foot three of agile power that once braced winds on the prow of the long boats, hacked and hewed Roman invaders blood red and once looked dragons eye to eye. Conveniently placed he sat with a slurred smile surveying the dance floor.

Meanwhile the band screamed his scream. The electronic wail of blood and battles tinged with the despairing shriek of gulls caught in a world without wind, floating languidly in an air conditioned asphalt dome. The cry of an animal bereft of seasons, cycles and instinct. The aimless beat of bird shit on temples. The grind and splutter of cogs, valves, machined technology and the piercing shriek of a lone human voice searching for the rain among boxed-in desperation and crowded loneliness.

As the fashion of the day decreed the dancers dressed, emphasizing their claim as mammals. Buttocks, crutch and milk secreting glands. Moving in accordance with the obsession of the technological age, a rhythmic thrusting cock grind, incorporating many lost sensations in an overstatement of one. Some danced for general approval while others danced specifically to excite the shaft of St George. A face almost handsome approved.

His father was a sullen man who had joined the army somewhat disillusioned with life after his seventh child died of neglect. Caused a quiet scandal at the primary school but its effects were largely cushioned because George, although a hopeless scholar was the star of the senior rugby tourney team. Behind a sullen expression George tumbled up alone in his suburban world of ragged hedges, state insulated battery boxes and Saturday morning conversations that grated as the motor mower whined.

If you've taken my spark plug spanner I'll break your bloody neck.
Now don't forget. Two large tins of spaghetti and a loaf of spare bread.
Who's taken the wringer off the washing machine?
Where's me rugby shorts?

Who pissed on the toilet floor?
If you don't shift that bike I'll run over the bastard next time.
You bloody kids get outside and play!
No its George, he threw Nephi Hall in the creek for the third Saturday running and she's threatened to get the welfare onto him.
The bloody ringer was down at Bells lying in the chicken house covered in shit.
I'll break his bloody neck!
Turn that bloody television down. I can't hear the first leg.
Mandy, get inside you stupid little bitch and stop that bloody whining or I'll give you something to whine about.

George found his armour early, floating among the sea of random probability. From the roller coaster jangle of child-street memories there jarred a mocking clarinet solo; *Georgie Withers is a sook,* with peels of circus laughter on a trombone.

Billy Watts was seven, bigger and heavier and waiting at the shops the afternoon George walked home with nothing on his mind other than the picture he had made from sawdust and glue. Billy ran into him from behind with his chain bike, knocking him down and skinning his knees. George began to cry, then run, while Billy, cheered on by a group of elders, punched him in the face and ripped his picture. George went sobbing home accompanied by a revelling group of players who danced and mocked, feeling secure because the cross was carried for them. Two minutes after his arrival came his elder brother Paul, shamed and chanting even more bitterly. Bloody little sook, said his mother, who understood the need for self defence better than any of them. Don't come crying to me. When I was your age I would have fixed him, said his father, who drank with Mr Watts. Get to your room and don't come out til you stop crying. If you could fight as well as cry you'd have licked the arse off him.

That night he wept a silent vigil, fasting and alone, straining for the sounds of his mother's footsteps and shrinking from the pain of the world. When the others came to bed he ignored the taunts, pretending to be asleep, pressing his finger into his blood furrowed knee to prove that he wasn't a sook at all.

Six months later I beat the shit out of Bill Watts. I grabbed a rock and smashed the mud guards on his chain bike. I threw the bell into an empty section and smashed out the spokes in the front wheel.

George was never accepted at school despite the efforts of the welfare system to keep him leaning forward into the waves. And you are dumb St George peeled the bells. Subjugation the whistles shrieked. Step lightly my lad from box to box and learn to live in the urban zoo. But where is your homework George? To the office my boy. God only helps those who help themselves. And George lay disarmed, pounded by wave after wave that thundered desks, rules, trivia, meaninglessness and skip to my loo upon his head. It certainly was true though that God helped him when he helped himself and he learned to steal what they wouldn't give him and punch those who said no. But the sting of the cane across his buttocks, the obsessive way he rode his genitals, a prow against the waves, taught him that the spirit lay elsewhere than the educated mind and he grasped for the ample tits of Louise Peters.

Hey George what a stink band. You can't even dance to that crap.
Yeah! I feel like hooking that little shit.

Fade from the floor. Rhythm fell away as the thrust and pound meandered into intricate patterns of fantastic inquiry. The subtle thrust of why penetrating through the repetitive pulse of cock grind. Varied time signatures explored and the piercing despair of a talented lead guitar, presenting lone metaphysical measures of loss, meshing against the cogs of rapid slide and the ever increasing madness of the machine, moving forward, straight ahead, butterflies splattered against the wheel. And the angels sang to you Oh George and you could have wept, except that warriors are strong and as the office blocks insulate the rain so the hedged boxes imprisoned your tears. Upward, upward soared the band as they jammed on, minds floating soft and warm in the gentleness of clouds blown from the last breaks joint.
Breathe fire dragon. Puff the heat from your belly.

A quarter past eleven with the atmosphere of flat froth and an early hangover round the bar. Prospects of nastiness because the band didn't play this week's top pops. A suspended grumble with patrons robbed of the final orgasm. That final hour, when with inhibitions drowned, George would have danced, Viking hair blown towards the stars. A dragon would have to be found.
When are they going to chuck that band out?
Let's get some piss for later. I'll fix them.
Let a dragon without claws feel the pain of my wrath.

Strop packed his guitar and pushed tomorrow from his mind. Another job lost. Didn't play the right stuff. People couldn't dance. Too many complaints from the customers. A simple problem, to play for money or art, but it was just the practicalities that were hard. Tomorrow was the day they had to leave their present flat. The neighbours complaining about the loud music late at night he understood as the euphemism for, I read in the paper that one of you was busted for selling cannabis sticks. Your hair is too long and you don't appear to work. Your socialisation appears fragmentary at best.

Strop understood that that was the way of it. There had always been something wrong with him. He was too sensitive as a child and had wept bitterly when they put his mother in an asylum after several suicide attempts. It seemed that life as a solo mother in a state block of flats had proved unbearable despite the weekly welfare cheque. Never fear my lad we'll get you into a decent home. His auntie found him as sly and insidious as she always knew he must be, coming from a more attractive younger sister, who may have got all the men but received her just desserts in the end. He had been too timid to play sport at school and too afraid of the cane to make many friends. Teachers Training College spoke for itself.

Sit down Mr Couper. I have just been reading over your records and it appears that you have had some difficulty adjusting to the standards of the institution, both academically and personally. What I think you need to realise is that you cannot underestimate the importance of appearances in the professional situation. Especially when you go out to your career and it will be necessary to mix with both parents and principals. If you appear unkempt and scruffy, then I am afraid you are just setting yourself up for failure. Do you understand what I mean? In creating a bad first impression you will be, in effect, selling yourself and us, as an institution, short. Now as we regard teacher's college as a training in both the academic and social spheres then I must inform you that unless you appear better groomed by the end of next week your acceptability will have to be reviewed by the terminating committee.

So I left. I just couldn't relate to it all. You know. It occurred to me that even in a new suit my balls would still itch. Or if I took out my liver and rinsed it under the cold tap it would still have been the same liver. Only cleaner. And bugger it, this is me. I sing and fart, warts and all.

So he played his guitar and smoked dope with other dragons, living in caves beneath the cities. Dope packed like cotton wool around the brain and promoted visions. Keep your eyes downcast Strop Couper. Withdraw to the safety of your insides for all about is pain. Meander on clouds of sound, soft and warm against the grey reality and never look down. Inside you are safe from the cog that grinds. Fetid, it sweats, seeping ooze, choking the rivers and coughing phlegm at the air. And the terrible tick-tock of its hunger as it reduces human flesh to production parts, which mourn the loss, but scurry to produce and peck disconsolately at the crumbs.

And if people look at me with fear in their eyes it is not because I am a dragon. My smoke is synthetic. My nostrils dribble snot upon my beard. It is self fear. Fear that the daily hallucinations of fragmentation and air conditioned panic are nothing more than a head diluted in a plastic bag. Fear that the age of cock has wilted. Mother I have chilblains on my testicles. Dragon it is not your claws I fear it is your visions, for I have television tubes in my eyes. Electricity help us when the vagina also runs dry. Float Strop Couper among your dreams.

I sometimes have this dream. It is raining. I stand in a field, knee deep in lush pasture and assorted wild flowers. The sun also shines, radiating the vivid colour, highlighting the passionate depth of the rain washed green. As I walk I notice that all manner of plants are sprouting, randomly, mocking time, growing as I watch. A herd of cows is there. I watch the bull on his rounds carefully assessing the precise moment to enter and with an ecstatic explosion of spring life animate the earth. Cross eyed, glazed and bestial he wastes a glance at me. Soft pad lips drooling saliva and cow juice. But back to business, sorry mister, too fucked to fight.

I realise that I am growing in time as the warmth penetrates my skin. I give myself over to the hypnotic rays of the sun, expanding upward and out. Evening birdsong grows louder. The soft kiss kiss note of the Tui, echoes water trickling and savoury swallows of honey dew. The intricate, elusive hurry of blackbird song, contrasted by the eerie, insect scraping of the warbler. Then from the swamp, penetrating all, the shriek of the pūkeko, signalling the neutral time, poised between evening and night. I stop growing. As the rain continues and the night sounds grow, I am washed away, melting like water colours, gently into earth.

The band gear was packed into the van as tired barmen confronted mountains of dirty glasses and hurried reluctant leavers out of the door to mill around in the car park, revving machines, hoping for parties, women and somewhere to go. Strop Couper sat hunched, feet on the dashboard, waiting for a joint to be rolled, before heading off for a bag of chips.
What shall we do now, said Chris.
Something will turn up, replied Strop, here.

The joint travelled round, rapidly disappearing down lungs with a higher probability of developing a bronchial condition than the national average. Hang on, I'll have a piss.
The night was cold. Black, ponderous clouds blew in foreboding shapes across an undernourished moon. Spots of rain fell, scattered by a wind that rattled empty beer bottles stacked in crates in the alley behind the bottle store.

And now, George blocking the alley. Faint smile, savouring surprise and dawning fear. Strop Couper, a vague sickness, moving dreamlike trying to edge past. I am St George. You have made me suffer, ruining the sacred pleasures of my Saturday night, self worship service. As a consequence I will sacrifice you dragon. I will draw blood from your nose, blacken your eyes and kick you in the guts as you lie retching on the ground. In the process I will shed the shame and futility of another week's pointlessness at the building site.

As in the days of old
I keep threats from my master's door
Whereas I once did it for pay
I do it now because I'm poor

And no hard feelings brother!
As they said in Auschwitz
Clawing at each others eyes
To get to the vents
And live
A second more

The White Horse Haka

We had just about worn out the goodwill of the Sunday morning. All the left over beer had been cleaned up from the night before. The men were cheerfully pissed, the sheila's had fed us with good grace but we had reached the point where the hospitality begins to wear thin. The only course left was to go back home and sober up to the persistent nagging of one's own domestic responsibilities. It had been a good weekend.

"Heh Pad! We should get some more grog," said Tiki.
Between the two of us we managed to steer the conversation on to that delicate matter. The complacent men were supportive, but in a short time it became obvious that if there was to be any more grog procured then Tiki and I would have to procure it. So we did.

Uncle Taki and Brownie put the hat round for a dozen and with still some grudging good will from the sheila's, we managed to procure a one way ride in the direction of the White Horse Tavern, near the Longburn Freezing Works. Pom and Tania dropped us close to the hotel, situated in a row of closed shops in the main street. There was not a sign of life from the hotel but we walked through the empty car park to the front door and rang the bell. Much to our encouragement we heard footsteps and the door was opened. A middle-aged, Pākehā barman looked with annoyance through the opened door. A man into rugby, racing and beer and not over fond of bloody Māori shit stirrers one bit. No, he was sorry but they did not sell alcohol on a Sunday. We would have to go somewhere else, he advised. I tried to reason with him. He firmly wished us goodbye and began to close the door. In desperation Tiki let fly a vigorous torrent of abuse and began to strut a haka, in the mode of a challenge on the Marae, except that he substituted foul threats in English for Te reo tikanga.

The man was taken aback by this, but being of stout stuff he stood his ground. Drawing some encouragement from the fact that he looked a bit paler, Tiki danced with greater animation and swearing profusely gave him another round. I saw fear beginning to grow. This man's quiet Sunday morning was disintegrating into an ugly, race riot rampage. I seized the opportunity.
"Look I tell you what, mate. Here's the money. Just put a dozen out the back door and we'll go quietly away. No more trouble."

I discerned immediately that he was struck by the wisdom of these words, offering as they did a face-saving solution. He quickly nodded agreement and I handed him the money. Tiki continued muttering curses and showing off his tats. The door closed and walking back out into the sunlit street we made for the back courtyard. It was one of those defining moments. He had the money and we stood locked out on vulnerable ground. Much to our relief we again heard footsteps, the sound of the door unlocking and our man emerged bearing a dozen large bottles of DB in a crate. I grasped the crate quickly and thanking him for his consideration we withdrew.

We knew we had won a great victory. We strode back down the road out of town with that crate between us. We lay down in the long grass beside the road and cracked a bottle, laughing uproariously. Victory tasted sweet and we poured it down. Exuding creative lunacy we had a wonderful time wandering that Sunday afternoon highway. Tripping on that alcohol-fired, adrenaline spark, we entertained each other with stories, jokes and reflections on life. We took the piss out of psychology and philosophy, celebrated spirituality and expounded our own reflections on the essence of being. We talked over scenes from great literature. We acted and laughed and drank our way down that sunny highway afternoon alternating speeches, song, poetry and dance like a mad chorus troupe from Brecht. There we were, about the time parents from my school took their kids for a family drive to the beach, cavorting drunk and disorderly at the side of a public road. While the crate was full, we cared not.

Towards late afternoon I vaguely recall calling into a house occupied by a university acquaintance of Tiki's. We were glad of a seat off the road and used the phone to try to con Pom into picking us up and giving us a lift back home. Although she was good natured she was also direct and told him we could piss off. By this time it was getting onto evening and what with the crate getting empty there was nothing for it but to set off into the lowering sunset in the direction of home.

Some hours later I startled awake to find I had been sleeping in the gutter of a suburban street in Palmerston. Staggering to my feet I discovered Tiki lying some yards further on. He awoke and we stood stupidly looking about. It dawned on me that we were only a few houses along from a friend who had lectured me at Teachers College. As the wind was beginning to get cold, I decided to risk seeking this form of sanctuary. We staggered off down the street to the house. Fortunately my friend wasn't there and his sixteen year old son let us into the house. He could see we were in a poor state and graciously fixed us up with some of his Dad's grog.

Tiki decided to exorcise the wrath of his hangover and began to bait the lad with talk that had a racial, insulting tone. A middle class white boy to take the piss out of. However, this lad was staunch working class from Birmingham and in the ensuing contest they both gained mutual respect. So much so that they decided to become blood brothers and taking up the bread knife hacked at each other's wrists until the blood mingled freely together and ran all over the kitchen bench.

While I was deeply touched by the unity expressed in the coming together of the two races, I also harboured visions of the father returning home to find me drunk and dishevelled in the company of an obtuse Māori, with slashed wrists dripping blood all over his son. I realised at that point that the party was finally over for that day and quietly slipping out the back door disappeared into the misery of a cold domestic night.

Leaving School

Patches of broken light flickered on the shelves through a small window set high in the cement wall. They illuminated the covers of faded welfare files, long unopened. Dead specks of dust arose in shafted columns, beginning the dance that yearned upwards towards the source. The dreams of the dead, escaping in clouds from the vaulted prison of the system. Kevin lying comfortably across a canvas bag of discarded receipt books. Smoke curling from his nostrils, joining in the dance as they caught the columns of light. Fumes of the mind, slipping through the cracks in the ceiling, to drift ecstatically with the caresses of the wind.

The sound of footsteps echoed purposefully down the concrete hallway. Kevin leaps from the sack, extinguishing the joint in the palm of his hand and turned to grasp a half empty sack of assorted rubbish. Meet the bastard outside, away from the pleasant smell of euphoria and dancing dreams. Outside the door, the man in charge. Small and grey, dressed in a light brown suit. Well presented and flashing a worn out smile.
"How's it going"?
"Yeah, good."
"Finding where everything goes alright?"
"Yeah."
"Listen, I see from your records that you're a teacher. Well, later this month we will be advertising two vacancies for social workers. I thought it might be a good idea for you to apply. There's not much future for a man of your education doing this relief work. What you ought to do is think about getting a good career for yourself. Something that will bring in some regular money and job security."
"Like being a social welfare officer?"
"Well I'm not saying that you would get the job, but it would be better than wasting away your life doing this kind of thing."
"I like this kind of thing. I'll think about it."

Kevin back on the sacks watching the minutes tick away until lunchtime. Smoke haze drifts up through the solitary window. A reminder of those other windows of assorted classrooms. Cold translucent shields blocking access to the outside world. Outside, the view of paddocks responding to the dripping caress of warm rain. Inside, the product of human caressing, regulated now with me the jailer.

We have to turn them out to be useful citizens that fit the system. We have to equip them with the kinds of skills that will enable them to play a productive part in the market place. We have to violate the free spirit of childhood. We have to make them prisoners of the man, until they learn the persistent dog trot of adulthood, shoulders against the wheel .Whining routinely like the suburban lawn mowers.

Kevin dying in classrooms. Like a goldfish with big eyes, staring through the window at the outside world. Reaching out for the vibrant pulse of life, the tantalising possibility of half- realised dreams. Is this all it is? A gold fish with expectant eyes staring through the glass at the vibrance of the rain and the distant possibility of a sunset.

He hadn't really considered it when he got up that day. It was so warm and beautiful. Spring was well advanced and the air was alive with the busy cacophony of bird song. He was late. Still slightly hung over from the night before, driving to school nearly an hour after the tolling of the bell. He knew they would be coldly hostile. Well, he'd been late before. Sometimes half a day late in Palmerston North. Walking down that long corridor with no one daring to say a word because they knew that he didn't even care. Afraid that he may say something altogether unexpected. Sensing that somehow he was playing the game by a different set of rules.

It was as the car pulled into the parking area beside the school. An inner voice spoke as though for the first time and flooded over him with a feeling of intense relief.

I don't have to do this. I only come here because I choose to. I can just stop!

Somehow he had become locked in under the chilling weight of their expectations. Expectations that he had begun to wear like a weighted dog collar. Kevin walks to the classroom.
"Kids, I've got something to tell you. I'm leaving today. I won't be coming back any more."
Little eyes shining with romantic wonder.
"Aw, aren't you going to finish that story you were telling us?"
He finishes the story. A made up serial tale about a Celtic hero from the old times. The hero rode out on adventures and wooed the heart of a beautiful princess. They drank in the tale, grabbing the dreams, fortifying themselves for a moment against the adult world of forced growth and constant expectation.

"Now be good. I'll go and tell Miss Harvey. You guys wait here until she sends someone. See you kids."

"Goodbye Mr Barry."

Walking across the yard to the principal's room. She, bristling and cold as he entered, trying to ignore him.
"I just came to tell you I'm leaving."
"What do you mean you're leaving? When?"
"Now. I'm off now. I'm going."
"You can't do that. You've at least got to stay until the end of the day."
"Sorry it has to be like this but I'm going. Now. Goodbye."
"But..... but."

Kevin crosses to the car taking just a small bag from a now meaningless assortment of educational paraphernalia accumulated over seven years. A few kids peer wide eyed from the classroom door. He waves, then starts the car and drives unhurried into the beautiful freedom of a Northland spring morning.

Later that day he rang the Education Board to organize his final pay.
"Oh! Mr Barry, we understand. Just write a letter explaining what went wrong and then you will be able to leave the door open for when you wish to return."
He tried to write but the biro was on its last legs. Finally he managed.

Dear Sir,
I'm writing to advise you that I'm leaving because my pen is rapidly running out of ink—

With that the biro sputtered to a stop.

Fish Webs

Down by the river, she sat under the bridge again. Shadows flickering through sunlit trees and rippling in the wind blown eddies. Invisible fish leaping onto grass smelling grassy banks looking for greener pastures and Rosy. Rosy very still, watching with her eyes to catch the silly fish leaping, but they avoided her pleas with a persistent stubbornness.

Rosy you get back home straight away or I'll tell your father... Rosy you spiteful little...you listen to what I say now... wait till your father gets home.

The fish didn't fool Rosy. It was the decree of the fish king that not everybody was able to see them as they leapt to the sunlight parading their glistening scales. But she knew that if you were someone special they would come and talk to you.

It is true Miss White. I saw them down at the river just like in that story. Don't be silly Rosy. That was only a made-up story.

Come on fish. I'm only a girl. Please let me see you.

The fish wouldn't be reasonable so Rosy walked along the bank with the grass bending and slithering to escape the doom of sodden feet. Mud squelching warmed her ears, shone her eyes but dirtied her best socks.

You ungrateful little... don't you know socks cost money... do you think money grows on trees... where have you been... how many times have I told you... how do you think you're going to get those clean... Rosy how do you think... Rosy Morris you get inside... Rosy Morris can you hear me.

I only went to see the fish.

The bridge. Stones, smooth and round, rolling away to reach the banks but stopped by engineers from the board. Hello Rosy came the voice from under the bridge. This is my bridge. You cannot walk on it.
Who said it's your bridge? You never made it because fish can't make bridges.
But I am the fish king, said the trout and to prove it he took his crown from his pocket.
That crown looks silly and I'm going to walk on your silly bridge see.

Guards! yelled the king with a smile and Rosy laughed too. Down through the silent water she was pulled handcuffed to a lobster's tail. In and out through seaweed trees, flashing stones and eyes.

Rosy this is a serious crime that you are charged with, said the judge, shuffling his wig. Insulting the king has never been done in the history of Skitesgrub. Rosy did feel a little ashamed and the orchestra only made it worse with twenty five water rats playing violins. But! said the judge, in the wrong key, we have decided to be very lenient (you could have split the silence with a fish hook) because you are so beautiful. With these words the waters rippled with the sound of cheers and Rosy's hair rose to the very top of the courthouse roof.

Please can I have one Jean? Only one. You've got all of those.
No! Why don't you get some off your own mother.
Mummy can't get me any. Oh please Jean. I'll let you play with my skipping rope.
I don't want your skipping rope. I've got my own anyway. Rosy Morris's mothers a meanie. She won't give her any lollies and she belts her.
She does give us lollies sometimes and she doesn't belt me.
Big liar Rosy Morris I've seen her ha!
Only when I'm naughty and anyway your mother's fat and she eats a rat.
Ha ha! Jean Wrights mother's fat and she eats a rat.
Rosy Morris you get home. Wait till I tell your mother. Go on and don't come round here again you only cause trouble with our Jean.

Rosy have you been fighting Jean Wright again... Rosy how many times...Rosy you get inside...how many times have I told you about fighting with Jean.

Miss White my father can't go to work anymore because of his leg and it won't be better for one year. I have to get up early in the morning and help mummy with the twins.
Never mind Rosy. Be careful that you don't knock that paint over.

Sitting with the fish king under the bridge. Rosy I have asked you to come here to play with my children. You will have to help them polish their scales, Oh and make absolutely sure that they don't play near the fish hooks.
I know you're a good girl Rosy, you always do as you're told.
Come on then fishes and if you're good, then I'll tell you a story.
We don't want to hear a stupid story. We want to go and play near the fish hooks.
Yeah we want to go and play near the fish hooks.

Come on Rosy, you've got to take us.
No! Your father said no. Now do as you're told. Come back here. Please come back, I can't swim as fast as you. I'll tell your father. Just wait till your father gets home.

Mummy when is Pauline going to have her baby? Will it be here soon? Rosy go away and play. Can't you see I'm busy.
But Mummy when is Pauline going to come back with her baby? Can she come soon? Why can't I tell Jean about the new baby or Miss White? Don't you like babies mummy? Why do they make you cry?

>Slowly the moon
>The fish
>And I

Rosy Morris you are the laziest child I have ever known. I just don't know what's wrong with you. You've been sitting there all day and how much have you done? Three lines. Alright, well you can stay in after school and finish off then.

Moonlight, moss green. Bees humming around golden flowers. Trees bowing to the breeze and keeping in time to the jewel box stream which sings the praises of Rosie. She sits on a honey coloured throne handing out ice creams with fingers that dazzle patchwork gold. One hundred trout sit along the bank begging her to dance for them. Rosie danced whirling higher and higher until her feet no longer touch the ground but float among the tree tops on blankets of mist. Hair drifting, eyes shining brighter than her fingers while the gaze of the trout eyes warm the air. And now, said Rosie when she was quite finished. I declare that from now on everyday will be a holiday and I will be the kindest and most beautiful queen that you have ever had.

A pale green room, with mottled ceiling. Scratched floors covered with child eaten, ink scrawled desks. Rosie sitting among her personal belongings. Her very own maths text and her very own story book in which she could write anything that Miss White likes. A tear trickles over p 54 and saturates the third equation. The clock sits suspended at 3:15.

Walking home along a road that had been used many times before. Slow plodding footsteps that have cut themselves off from the brain and move as only feet know how. She trudges past Mr Fosters shed dark and closed.

Jean do you know what Mr Foster does in there all day? He has a secret way of making gold and he boils it up in a great big pot and then when he's left it for a few days he spins it into a golden web. One day he gave me a golden web necklace and Mummy told me that it's worth a hundred dollars.

You big liar Rosy Morris! Mummy told me not to listen to your stupid stories. Anyway she told me that Mr Foster is a carpenter and that he makes chairs. Anyway the Fosters have only got an old car because they are poor.

That's because he's kind and he gives all his money away to other people and I've even seen smoke coming out of the chimney. Anyway my mother told me that stories are what make the world go round.

Miss White if you know the secret can't you spin a golden web?
No Rosie, gold is found in the rivers or under the ground.

Rosy...Rosy where have you been...I've been out looking for you everywhere...look at your socks...come inside before you catch cold...where have you been?

Mummy I ran away from school and I went down to see the fish at the river. Mummy where's Dad.

Cabbage Sunday

One grey Sunday afternoon he caught the bus out to Graham's place. Staring out the window on a windswept afternoon to alight at the bus stop at Anderson's Bay and walk up the hill to his street. Year's earlier they had taught together at the Area school. Graham had caught his eye by exhibiting a creative mad streak. A big man with a ragged beard and one gammy leg, limping determinedly from place to place like a lame sparrow. His Friday night pub behaviour had been a highlight. As he got drunker he turned from a quiet, inoffensive misfit into a gross extrovert and insulted the rest of the staff with foul and offensive talk. His particular highlight included standing on the tables and spilling beer (never his own) over the table and giving his'"Fuck the System Speech," with articulate flair. On a number of occasions Kevin had led him home to escape irate publicans before all hell broke loose.

Graham staggered in the door.
"Bloody useless bastards. They're scared shitless to buck the system in case they lose their jobs. Couldn't give a fuck about the kids, all they can think about is their superannuation. Still got their empty heads stuck up their arses in Dickensian mode."
"Shut up man. Keep your voice down, you'll wake up the missus then we'll both be in the shit."
Kevin peering furtively down the corridor towards the bedroom. He had only seen the missus from a distance but from comments Graham had made he pictured her as a sulky bitch who spent her time sick and complaining in bed. Not the sort he wanted to tangle with at 7 pm on a Friday night when there was a good party to go to.

"Take it easy man, you'll be alright. I'd better get going so I can get a feed."
"What the fuck are you going for; we can have a feed here."
"No it's alright man I'd better be off. I'm late enough home now."
"I'll get you a bloody feed."
"For shits sake keep your bloody voice down, you'll not only have the missus onto us but the bloody neighbours will be kicking up as well."
"Fuck the bloody neighbours," with his voice raising a couple of levels. He staggers to the back door, slips over a half-empty washing basket, then pulling himself up manages to open it.
"Why don't you fucking bastards mind your own business?" he yells into the dark. "Bunch of bloody imperialist arseholes. I suppose you're the shit heads who voted to send the troops to Vietnam. Get yourselves an honest

bloody job instead of pestering the shit out of a half starved artist like me."
"Get inside you bloody idiot, you'll have the cops around here next."
"Fuck the cops. Bloody fascist pigs. Do you want a feed man?"
Graham lurches to the bench banging open cupboards and pulling food out of the refrigerator. A dish of leftovers crashes to the floor.
"Class I told you to line up inside the door —" and he does his high pitched maniacal laugh.
"There man I'll cook us a bloody feed."
He finds a couple of eggs in the refrigerator and with a triumphant laugh cracks them straight onto the element of the stove — no pan. A smell of burnt egg and Graham's laughing and swearing rising to a crescendo.
Kevin takes a final glance in the direction of the passageway. Bugger you Cameron, its every man for himself now.
"See ya mate, I'm off."
"What the bloody hell are you going for?"
Graham lurches after him but unfortunately tangles up and slips again over the washing basket by the back door as it closes and Kevin escapes into the night.

At the end of that year they parted, heading to other schools, and the years quietly slipped away. Today he got off the bus in a suburban street interspersed with patches of wilderness running diagonally across the hill. Light drizzle falling, driven by a chilling wind. Finally reaching the house, back lightly bent against the wind, trudging with a bag of memories, wondering what lay behind the empty windows. A cracked path of patchwork weeds, led past an autumn veggie garden, with a few spindly cabbages braced on careworn stalks. He remembered the poem he had written that Graham had illustrated

Cabbage
you are beautiful,
slobbering in the wind,
with your washstand wisdom
conical and bloated.

Cabbage,
you are like a cabbage,
ripe and split,
spreading your seed
on the earth that you have left uneaten.

You threaten me cabbage
with your dedication.
Green leaves, flapping cradle cruel
with the forces
you cannot understand.

Cabbage cavalier
skyward eyes
crawling earthworm;
yet you thrive
ejaculating your seed with the wind.

He knocks and Graham stands smiling at the door. Still the sparrow, keen-eyed with a determined hop, ready to pounce and pick up the discarded winter crumbs. The missus appeared to have undergone a recent metamorphosis, appearing plump, attractive and talkative. Like a naked snail, slithering out of her shell, to dine the more succulently on the fat of the cabbage.
"Yes, I'm now in charge of the senior classes and I'm hoping next year to apply for the assistant principal's job," said Graham after dinner.
"If you can't beat em, join em," with a self conscious laugh.
"What have you been doing? Are you still writing?"
"Oh yes, now and again," and he thought of the rolled sheet of papers lying back at the caravan park, sharing his only bag with yesterday's underpants and a couple of crumpled shirts. Maybe he just carried them for security to remind himself who he was. Not ordinary obscurity for him and he had the pieces of paper to prove it.

He looked at Graham sitting comfortable in his lazy boy rocking chair, gammy leg lazily spread before the heat of the gas fire. The house was ordinary but comfortable, insulated from the cooling wind. While the missus cleared away the remains of a commodious Sunday roast, he looked at his own reflection in the phoney, gilded lounge mirror. He saw long hair and good looks with a touch of sadness. A slight scowl that burst at times into the warmth of a smile. His old black woollen coat lay discarded over the lounge chair, revealing worn jeans and a grey woollen freezing worker's jersey. His emptiness was visible from the outside, worn like a patch on his lightly stooping shoulders, occupying the same spot as the recently ditched family and suburban bit.
Graham's emptiness appeared less obvious. He had tried to camouflage it with a veneer of respectability and the daily aspirations that kept the gas fires burning. A necessity inherently gleaned from his Scottish, working class pragmatism. But it was a fire that burned synthetically from the

outside, warming only the skin and all the while dousing the real fire that slumbered within the heart.

The Missus disconcerted him with an over-exuberance and outgoing vivaciousness that he remembered as uncharacteristic. Blonde hair, cut to curl around the base of the neck, framing a pleasant face. Her skirt, too short, revealing plump, succulent white thighs. He saw the fat body of the slug sliding across the stalk of the cabbage. A slug spreading its erotic slime and penetrating with its elongated head until it had eaten from the heart. She talked and laughed loudly treating him as though they had been great friends when in truth he had hardly known her.
"You're not going to meet a boyfriend tonight," said Graham with his maniacal laugh. Such remarks he found perplexing.

Kevin slept fitfully that night in the spare room, tightly curled under a duvet cover that barely kept out the cold. The morning came, punctuated by the sounds of domestic preparations from the living area as the family contended with the realities of the new week. He heard the door bang and the sound of the car as Graham drove off to the classroom. Shortly after, the door opened and the Missus flounced in, dressed in a red silk bath robe, robustly settling a cup of tea beside the bed and loudly explaining that she was running him a bath and that it would be ready soon. He glanced at her ample breasts falling between the robe and last nights comments about boyfriends began to hazily focus.
He felt strangely irked. He didn't like being ordered about and began to shrink inside protecting his space. After the cup of tea she called out that the bath was ready and so to keep the peace he walked through to the bathroom, undressed and slipped beneath the warmth of the water. The door opened and the Missus walked in, the bathrobe was now unbuttoned and he caught a rounded stomach and curled pubic hair between sensuous white thighs.
"I thought you might like your back scrubbed," she announced over loudly, looking meaningfully down into the soapy mire. He felt himself withdraw, caught unprepared. For him it was all wrong. Only a casual laugh or risqué remark and the deal would have been clinched but his feelings couldn't be forced. It was all too fast. He saw only a stranger, with the thighs of a slug, seeking to envelop him with perfumed slime. He saw Graham in the classroom. He felt his own domestic strife and heart still raw from the encounter. He looked at her.
"No it will be ok, thanks."
 Their eyes met, and as she looked into his determined withdrawal the confidence ebbed. Feeling embarrassed she left the room.

Confessions from a Rabbit Hunter

In a dawning realization their eyes locked. What if he has drowned? We will be free to love one another. They knew also, that both of them had reached that same awareness. Her face, fresh in the late morning breeze, looked at him with intense longing, eyes shyly down. He found it hard to move for a moment, and with a wave of desire, fully believed that he could now have her to love openly. They had been handed a beautiful gift on this sunny morning by the sea. A gift from the hand of death.

A seabird squawk startled his reflection and he became conscious of the moderate swell surging rhythmically against the rocks. A light spray danced in the sunlight blending with the mist. A babble of gulls squawked as they argued over a piece of fish bait. But where was Alan? It must have been all of thirty minutes since they had seen him disappear around the side of the rocks, swimming through the cold swell to reach the largest mussels. He turned to her again. She met his gaze with a new openness. Desire blended with hope. He felt the strength leave his legs and half sitting against a rock outcrop, he took her again with his eyes, remembering that first look.

On a Monday morning two weeks ago, he had caught the bus from Dunedin to St Clare and Alan had met him at the bus stop. They hadn't seen one another for fifteen years, when they had lived as childhood neighbours and played rugby together on front lawns. Alan hadn't changed much. He just looked older. Kevin had wondered how Alan would handle the way he looked. He supposed he had the look of someone who was either a university student or a long haired layabout and he didn't think either option would appeal much to Alan.

Getting off the bus, they shook hands and experienced that distanced strangeness of knowing one another very well. Alan seemed friendly, and throwing the bag in the back of the van they set out to drive to his home.
"And what do you do for a living now?" Alan inevitably asked.
Kevin smiled to himself as he answered. "Oh I was teaching up until a couple of months ago, but at the moment I'm taking a holiday."
He felt the answer had a settling effect and knew that it put him closer to the academic end of the spectrum. By the time they reached Alan's place they were comfortable together, talking of other kids they had played with in the street. He noticed that Alan, being two years older, still assumed an authoritative edge in the relationship.

"Come and meet the family," said Alan, as they finally pulled up to a simple bach, across the road from the sea. Alan's mother had mentioned, disapprovingly, that Alan had married a black woman during the time he had lived in Nigeria and that when he had moved back to New Zealand he had brought her and her two teenage kids with him. As Kevin walked inside, with his well travelled canvas bag across his shoulder, she was standing at the sink with her back to him. She turned awkwardly and their eyes met. His gasp was inaudible. She was beautiful. Long legged with pronounced African buttocks, wearing a lightly clinging skirt. Her skin was very dark and her face attractive with large eyes. She smiled shyly, but held his gaze. As he continued to stare momentarily into the deep well of her eyes, he watched her first look of shy surprise flicker into an open stare of deep longing. There was a sweet sadness in those eyes that looked at him now with an open invitation. Fill my need. Finally looking away, they were both consciously aware that a look of desire had passed between them. Disconcerted, he sat at the table and made conversation with Alan and the kids.

Over the next week he lived comfortably at Alan's and fitted into the family routines. The two kids were pleasant to get on with, and as Alan worked from home as a mechanic, he was able to make time during the day to take Kevin on excursions around the old neighbourhood. He enjoyed Alan's company again discovering the same humorous but calculating edge. Together they lived a childhood part of themselves, sharing memories.

In the cold of the winter evenings, as the southerly began to blow around the back of the garage, Alan and one of his mates often spent time lying under various vehicles fixing them. Kevin would enter the cottage, after excusing himself with jokes about the cold, and the softness of Northlanders. Inside the house she had the coffee hot beside the fire. He produced a bottle of brandy from the pocket of his black coat and poured two generous dollops into the cups. They stirred honey into the drinks and sat talking together. She was the daughter of a man who was an important warrior in a small African village. The men of the village were lion hunters. She told him that once her father had walked into an enclosure, and with one blow from his bare fist had felled a full grown bullock.

Now she shivered slightly before this fire. Outside, the southerly blew across the open maram grass and her husband lay on the concrete under a vehicle in the garage. Inside before the warmth of the fire, a kindly stranger reawakened that womanly part of her. That desire to be listened to and taken seriously. To feel attractive. To see the hunger of desire in a man's eyes. A spirit of love and understanding melted the crippling loneliness in her heart. For too long she had worn out the smile at the Rugby Club, among that hard chauvinistic world of Kiwi pragmatism. She no longer wanted to know the Saturday score or about the ruptured diff lock in the van. She wanted her heart to be nurtured.

Suddenly Kevin had to do some serious thinking. He was certainly strongly attracted to her, caught by her dusky beauty and mysterious animal spirit. If only he could spend time with her alone. He desired nothing more than to hold her in his arms and give her that protective, gentle love that welled within him. At the same time there was the problem of Alan and the kids. His own recent pain of domestic rupture still sat heavily upon him. He was both energised and overwhelmed by the situation.

One wet night he went through the usual goodnight jokes about the cold and retired to the house. He smoked one of his few remaining joints and they sipped the coffee mixed with honey and brandy. The room was warm with a good log fire. Outside, the wind moaned across sand swept maram and the seabird squawks, gusted eerie, before a starlit half moon. He felt lovingly ebullient as brandy and fire lapped over him. She sat before him and with urgently beautiful face, offered herself to him. He supposed it was the way it was done around African fires. She simply said

"From now on I will be your women and go where you go."

"What about the kids?"

"The kids are old enough to look after themselves now. They will be alright staying here."

"But where shall we go?"

We have to go forward like the lion hunters, holding our fate in the skill of our hands."

"But I'm only a rabbit hunter," he smiled, thinking of his own shooting up north.

He fell silent and looked at her. She was highly intuitive, speaking her mind, unfettered by the social mores that bound him. Her life force flowed from another world exuding a strong animal femininity. Having lived closer to nature she mirrored the random eccentricity of wild fate. Grasping each new day she was able to fly with the current. Drifting as the search might take her. Gently clasping her hand he gazed at her, overwhelmed. She seemed too big for him. He saw the difficulties. How could he do this to the family? Where would they go?

That wet night, as the wind crashed the sea against moon glazed rocks, they stood before the fire, about to kiss, when the door opened and Alan came in, looking agitated. Kevin reacted within a split second and fluidly turning, picked up his drink which lay on the mantle piece. He created the impression that they had just passed momentarily, in normal movement across the room. Turning, he looked fully in the face of Alan. Alan was pissed off. Anger precariously balanced. Eventually, he averted his eyes and barked instructions at his woman who followed him into the bedroom.

And now today, the day before Kevin was due to catch the bus into Dunedin and leave town. A bright but cool, blustery day. Alan, in a good mood, suggested the trip down to get the mussels. The family fell in with him and they headed out to a rocky outcrop on the coast. Kevin and the woman were too enveloped in their own concerns to be sure how long Alan had been gone. Suddenly they knew they were alone. Then the dawning look. He has drowned. We are free to love one another. Inflamed desire given free rein, knowing that now it could be physically consummated. He leaned against the rock, feeling weak.
"Where the bloody hell have you been?"
It was Alan stamping around the edge of a rocky outcrop, wet and shivering. He did his block.
"You were supposed to be waiting with the bloody sack so I could put the mussels in. What the bloody hell were you doing?"
They looked sheepish. Caught out. Kevin and Alan looked at each other. It was suddenly like those other times on the front lawn. Those times when Alan decided who would play on who's team and who would do the kick off. Habitually Kevin picked up the kit of mussels and followed as Alan grumped off ahead. She followed slightly behind. He stopped and looked at her, tragic disappointment but release in his eyes. She looked back with sadness and frustrated longing. Trudging again to bend her back before that ache of loneliness in her heart. He caught the bus out of town that day and went north, but he never forgot. Years later, on the day that he killed his first wild boar, he thought of her and wondered how it might have been different.

A Bush Night Out

And then we came to Mamakau. The sponge of the North. Hot, wet and vibrant. Isolated. Kathleen had applied for a terms relieving at the area school and after the first day she told me that there was a job teaching math in the secondary dept. Dutifully I went for an interview, informing the principal that math was my worst subject and that I hadn't coped beyond form two level. It didn't matter he said, with a furtive look, so reluctantly I took the job.

Figuring to save on the rent we moved into a derelict, rat infested house beside a small stream, just up an overgrown back road. The place was rotten and beyond any usual habitation, but we set off a borer bomb to kill the insects, and the bee hive and moved our few belongings in.

The principal's look was as good as his word. It didn't matter much. The form 3-5 classes weren't interested in math either, so we settled into a comfortable, don't hassle me and I won't hassle you routine. They made a pretence of working through math texts while we played guitars and talked of other things. That principal was an enigma. Very articulate but strange eyed. I didn't understand until the night I saw him late at the local pub, incoherently drunk. It turned out he went every night after school and ate away his self esteem, camouflaging it during the day with furtive glances. Liquid eyes fearing exposure.

The deputy principal was mad. A Scottish immigrant, who crossed over into the other world when telling the kids off at assembly. His voice would rise to a fiery, impassioned crescendo as he worked himself up to his usual coup de grace.
"I've taught all over the world. I've taught in more countries than most of you could manage to name. All over the world I've been teaching school and ....." Working himself up now so that his eyes pulsated red darts as he devoured them with his malevolent glare.
"... and then I came to Mamakau and a more useless bunch of no hopers I've never found anywhere."

Apollo was doing odd jobs at the school and one Friday afternoon, in late winter, Kathleen informed me that we had been invited to stay at his place for the weekend. I had seen him occasionally around the school but had never spoken to him. He was tall, with long straggly blond hair and he had a large koru tattooed across each cheek. Kathleen had talked with his wife Rewia who invited us to stay. After school we packed a few clothes in a bag and drove down the road towards Waipipi. It was late in the afternoon with a wet chill in the air. High rain clouds sat brooding heavily, encompassing the land with eternal greyness. The road to Waipipi was gravel and mud intersected by large potholes that yawned like discarded bomb craters. The old Hillman chugged up the hills and crashed down on the suspension as we swerved to avoid them.

"Where did you say they lived?"
"Oh I don't know, she said it wasn't far down this road and that they would wait for us at the turn off."
"What did he say?"
"I wasn't really talking to him. It was Rewia that invited us."
"Did he know we were coming?"
"Well I suppose so."

I began to sense that I had been put into a situation of someone else's making. It turned out he didn't know. Twenty kilometres later, when we got to the turn off he approached the car. He had shed his white overalls and now dressed in a green bushman's shirt with a large hunting knife hanging from a finely crafted belt. He looked irritable as he approached.
"I don't really think this is a good idea."
"What's that?"
"Coming to stay with us. We only have a little shack in the bush and we have to cross the river and walk in."
"Well we can hack the conditions, but we won't come if you don't want us too. It's up to you."
He gave me a long hard look. Maybe he saw something.
"I suppose if I rip the table out we'll have room. We had better get moving before it gets too dark."

We drove on through various paddocks and gateways until we parked on the banks of the Waitotara River, just below where it tumbled out of the bush clad gorge to the Waipipi flat. It was starting to rain steadily as we gathered with our gear on the bank. Apollo had disappeared upstream and returned leading a large black mare. I had my first look at Rewia. She was an attractive Māori woman, slightly on the plump side. The oldest daughter was twelve, a beautiful, dark bush nymph. The boy was nine, wiry with a cheeky grin.

They loaded up the horse with Rewia, the two year old and the split sacks with the groceries. The black mare plunged into the stream, turgid and muddy after the recent rains. There was a thirty yard stretch to cross and it came up to the mare's flanks splashing up her belly as she slipped occasionally on hidden rocks. Apollo, now naked from the long bush shirt down, waded in leading the rest. I took off my trousers and carrying footwear and bag followed. It was only running sluggishly and at worst up to the waist. I sensed Apollo watching, but we knew how to cross rivers.

A muddy track, punctuated with variable rocky outcrops, led along the far bank up river. Apollo was becoming politely hospitable as we trudged up the track, in the rapidly fading light and steady rain. Finally a short, steep path through mānuka, running directly up the hill, into a small sloping clearing. The cabin grew out of the ground at the upper end of the slope. It was 9ft by 6 ft, made of roofing iron, with an outside chimney on one wall. We waited in the rain, while Apollo beginning to laugh and joke now, took an axe inside, chopped up the table and dragging it in pieces flung it outside. Inside the cabin, taking two thirds of the total length was two sets of bunks along each wall. The other third was the now cleared space, where the table had been, in front of the fire.

While the kids lay about on the bunks Margaret and I sat on the floor with Apollo. The floor was made of hardened earth, covered with several layers of prime cattle skins stretched across the space before the fire. Rewia sat next to the fire feeding it and with a few cooking bowls and a bucket of water, prepared tea. Apollo, now quite affable, settled back with a hot coffee and began to tell his story.

He was a Norwegian seaman who 10 years earlier had immigrated to NZ. He came with an eagle tattooed across his chest, and the restless striving's for adventure that characterized his forebears. After getting the best from Auckland, during the time of full employment he moved up north to live in a teepee. He worked hard at hunting with bow and gun and grew crops to supplement the food. His grandfather had taught him to work horses and he used these for power and transport. In those days the cry was for self sufficiency. Make it yourself and then you are not dependant on the system. For some years he had lived the alternative lifestyle but was presently in a half way state, sometimes staying in Mamakau for work and coming back to the cabin in the weekends.

Apollo was now happy and relaxed. He had rubbed himself with oil and stripped to a loincloth as he talked beside the fire. A leather waistcoat revealed a silver medallion hanging from his neck on a chain. His hair was long and straight, parted at the forehead with a head band, framing the circular koru's tattooed across his cheeks and he wore the hunting knife in his belt. The smell of a cooked pancake mix was now emanating from the pan in the fire as Rewia giggled and joked her way through her domestic chores. Looking around I noticed that the cabin was lined with hardboard, and painted the earth colours of circular, American Indian symbols, The bunks and furniture were carved out of native saplings and flickered in the firelight. It was now raining very heavily, thundering down on the tin outside. The only light came from a kerosene lantern and the fire. We shared a large pipe full of marijuana with quiet ceremony and then ate from plates placed before us. Fresh hot pancakes, smoked eel, mullet and shop treats.

Sometime after the dinner chores had been done I rose and left the cabin to urinate. It was a black starless night with steady rain still falling. Away to the left the Waitotara had changed its sluggish song to a fully orchestrated roar. Apollo followed me outside and we stood together several metres from the cabin door. Inside we had been talking about our experiences in the drug scene and as we stood together I happened to mention that I liked acid. A splash of light from the open door fell across his face as he turned a sharp look upon me.
"Strange you should say that, because I was given some today."
"Why don't we drop it?" I replied, without thinking.
"What now?"
In the dark I shrugged, "well yeah."

The LSD was two tiny blue capsules shaped like cones. Inside Apollo cut them carefully into halves with a razor blade and we swallowed them. A curious trust now bonded us. With the swallow of the pill we entered another reality. Knowingly stepping into a small boat together, on the edge of the river, in the blackness of night, pushing nonchalantly into the stream. Which way would the boat drift? The gentle water of the eddies, or the roar of the current. Without oars we waited for the acid to bite.

A lightening shaft illuminated the cabin in electric light, freeing the tattooed korus to spin, momentarily. A deafening thunderclap followed instantaneously, then more heavy rain drumming on the tin roof. The cabin swirled gently, flickering warmly in the firelight. The smell of mānuka smoke protectively enveloping. A circular American Indian picture on the wall began to revolve, drawing me in. Four women, symbolizing the seasons of nature and life. The cabin walls pulsating gently, breathing the eerie half light of dancing, flickering flames. The picture revolved, pulsating incessantly, drawing us in like dice board players. Painting its own pictures of our past and future.

First came the green spring maiden, arising from the eastern sun. Gently nurturing the promise of beginnings. I saw Apollo, impulsive and brave, exercising the warrior spirit astride the quick gelding. Echoes of that far time, when with sword and shield fashioned from wood, he had fought with boys among the tombstones of the long dead ancestors who had sailed the long boats. Now in this new land of bush clad hills, fighting with dog and gun, he brought in the wild boar. I felt the touch of bare feet upon the earth, running vigorously through the profusely flowering mānuka. A Kererū flying high to the sun dived and swooped in play. Lovers splashing naked in the invigorating morning water, embracing the dew drops of cleansing promise. The land, the succulent womb of Papa, our earth mother. Embrace the mystical spirit of nature. Baptized and cleansed in the sperm of Rangi, the sky spirit. Smoke the sacred weed and feel the rhythm of the earth's breathing. Sex, young and impulsive. The sudden hot, wet flush of Rewia surging forth in birth. Children, brown and strong, astride the saddle or running barefoot through the still wet, early grass. The river, cold from the winter cleansing, invigorating to impulsive deeds. This spring will nurture strong love until the chicks fly in the end from the nest into summer.

Early in the morning the Ruru calls. Rewia hears, but refuses to listen.

The summer maiden, rose from the board emanating warm assurance. She wore the lazy blue of summer pleasure, adorned with a scattered profusion of rata flowers snow dusted white. The lazy warmth of the river, relaxing, eel full. By now the whare is built and the firewood plentiful around the cooking stones. The garden thrives in the good wet of earlier times. Time to pause and watch the bee, pollen laden, caress the luxuriant petals to suck more greedily at the nectar of life. Time for the horse riding, diamond flecked through the river. Time to stop and notice the rich laughter of the maiden, as she emerges from the waterfall, jewel drops of transparent innocence. Apollo rubs his body in oil and attends the huis of optimism and dreams run by the hippies and radical Māori. Resplendent in the warrior flower of manhood. Eyeing lustily the soft round curves of the women dressed for summer ripeness. Talking of the hunts and horse tales, swapping the wisdom of living off the land with boasting and self aggrandizement. It is warm and well fed in the sun.

The Ruru calls strongly in the cool of the early evening and Rewia begins listening to songs of another world.

In the firelight the cabin danced and moved, humming its protective song of warmth, while outside the rain and the river's awesome roar.

The shapes and colours lived and breathed. The carved warrior brownness of the bed poles pulsate before the ripe breasts of the autumn harvest maiden. See her come with laden splendour, buxom and mature, to give bountifully from the fruits of her womanhood. The glorious reds and golds enhance maturity. She gives, she gives, nurturing from sensuous depths, plump and succulent as the miro tree. The sun still caresses the land with warmth, gently waning. The birds feed busily in preparation for leaner times. The Kererū clumsily flaps, well fed among the tree tops. The food is gathered before the rains, falling softly at first. The love making satisfies deeply. Moving now from the physical embrace of summer, to drink deep draughts from the maturity of emotion. Yet with sadness too, for it can now be quantified and they begin to notice limitations. Now you reap only as much as you have sown and no more than that can be gathered, for winter comes.

The ruru is more frequent now, calling urgently in the night and Rewia listens with growing disquiet, worn with the mouths to feed and the endless chores.

All too quickly the cabin warmth diminishes and the light is obscured as the winter hag emerges, lined and careworn. A chill weaves its invisible mist among the blackened walls. The Kererū sits saturated, under the leaves, no longer beckoned in flight by the sun. The sensuous nights fade before urgent mornings that make shrill demands on tired bones and aching joints. How much work we must do to live this way! And the suck of the summer melon turns to bitterness. Apollo sits smoking in the cabin, dreaming of the things he will do after the endless list of chores.

Tauntingly now the ruru sings its urgent songs of death.

Rewia can listen no more so she turns to run, then half slips through the door, as the knife from Apollo's belt quivers in the wall where her heart had been. The ruru fades and Rewia beholds only the horned goat, waiting for her outside and she screams, gesticulating wildly. Who wants a mad thing that has begun to dwell in the other world? She is pushed like a useless thing from the warmth of the nest. Helpless now she lies exposed beneath the precise tapping of the judge's hammer. Wearing a black cloak and mumbling incantations he severs the children she has suckled from her sagging breasts. She is left to wonder alone, through the streets of the city, broken and emptied.

Sometime just after the dawn cock crowed, Apollo indicated the bunk with a smile. Make full use of the acid he smiled knowingly. Kathleen and I ate of the warm colours of love, gently enveloped by the secrecy of the blanket. Apollo spread an extra skin on the floor and lay with Rewia before the dying fire. Later that afternoon we returned down the road to the school at Mamakau.

In the Beef Market

Now it suddenly wasn't so certain. For the first time the reality of the project struck him with some force. From the moment he began, with a light urging from desperation, to pick out the one to shoot. One from the small, alert group of cattle on the hillside. They stood a mixture of defiance and concern as they faced the group of three humans. They faced the one with the gun, who looked urgently - which one to shoot?

Kevin had only a vague idea of the reality of the task when they set out that morning.
Late the night before they had agreed,
"Let's get a feed of beef for a change."
So they laid their plans and set out early, while the dew was still wet and the mist rose in patches as they alternated their way up bracken and mānuka hillsides. Mānuka that dripped the prismatic jewels of a succulent dawn.

With the gun, he led up the hill into the rolling basin, which looked over the valley and the river below. The cattle were bunched in a slight depression, close below the bush covered crown. They turned now from their morning grazing and faced with concern the approach of the humans.

They all looked so big to him. He had left with the vague picture of a 6 month old calf which hadn't seemed too bad to handle. Of course it was now into the winter and the six month old calves were closer to yearlings and in this particular mob most of them were full grown cows. A black and white one, seeming a bit smaller than the others, caught his eye as he scanned the group. It ran a little towards them, skittering, and stopped some forty yards away, head on.

He sat down supporting the rifle on his knees as he began to concentrate on the shot. He found the sight in the v and lined it up with the centre of the forehead. The 22 magnum shot, he anticipated, would drop the beast unconscious, leaving him to finish it off with the knife.

Carefully and precisely he fired the shot. He saw a judder go through the beast. A sudden explosion of shock as the bullet shattered bone on its forehead. But it didn't go down. It simply stood there, making the occasional step, with a hint of a stagger. For all outward appearances, it faced its attacker as resolutely as before. He aimed again and fired. This time he was sure he saw blood spurt from the nose as the beast shook its head and took, faltering steps forward. Staggering momentarily, it regained its footing and continued to face its attacker with a wild, defiant look. Lurching forward it jogged down and across the hill face towards the mānuka. He aimed again with his last shell, and fired. The beast kicked back as it was hit but continued at a run into the shelter of the trees and disappeared.

He knew now how serious it was. Here was one of his neighbour's cattle, running around with three bullets from his gun and he knew he had to find and kill it. If he failed, the carcase was likely to be found by the stockman that looked after the cattle. Without a word he started at a run in pursuit of the beast, kicking himself for only bringing three shells for the project. The others followed him as he ran into the mānuka, at the spot into which the beast had disappeared.

He cast around, criss-crossing the cattle tracks in the scrub, with eyes straining the shadows. It was almost by mistake that he found it, but suddenly there it was, backed into a small patch of scrub facing him. It was showing signs of the gunshot wounds. Blood ran freely from its nose and it staggered visibly on its feet. Now he was close. Reaching for his bowie knife he gingerly advanced. It bellowed, sending a flecked plume of crimson blood from its nostrils. He closed in with the knife, while it faced him, with a kind of desperate incomprehension. Then it ran. Vigorously it kicked out and charged. He stepped aside late, and the hand holding the knife slashed wildly past his own chest as it knocked him sprawling in its frenzied flight. The grim humour of the situation picked him up. It had knocked him arse over kite, nearly stabbing him with his own knife. He was determined now that he would kill it. He followed through the soft autumn mud of a slippery cow track.

Again he came upon the beast, not too far away, in a denser stand of tall young mānuka trees. Leaning heavily with sides heaving, blood dribbled profusely from its nose and it was swaying unsteadily. Heaving, mud-stained belly and head swinging as though to shake away the pain. He knew he had to be careful now and gripping the knife firmly, he stalked the distance. Keeping to one side of it he waited for the break. With a bellow and weary kick of the heels it came at a heavy run. Turning aside he moved up close to the heaving flank. Grabbing its closest foreleg he lifted it clear. Positioning his boot at the same time behind the other leg he leaned his weight against the flank and threw it over. It bellowed and rolled on its side on the ground. It was losing strength now. Grabbing the head he forced it back, leaving the neck revealed and taut. He cut down with the knife, just at the base of the throat and blood spurted forth. A symbol of his own flood of feelings. Grim satisfaction and relief.

Down in the valley the sun was beginning to shine with mid morning vigour, pushing away the last of the darker patches as it advanced into the gullies. A few dogs barked far off. He rested a moment, thankful that the beast lay still. Kathleen approached with Martin, carrying some packs, a spade and a saw. Although wanting to rest longer, he picked up the bowie knife and slit the skin, exposing the stomach. Plunging in his hands he dragged the bag and innards out onto the ground. Grasping both back legs he dragged the beast further down the hill, and began to slit the skin from around them.

Martin started to dig a hole in the clay, among the mānuka, to hide the remains of the beast. Then again dogs barked. This time he registered a vague unease. He began to listen and contemplate the possibilities. Over the next five minutes, while he skinned, the barking grew in volume, until it began to sound so close it threatened to explode onto the scene in a sudden mixed cacophony of excited barks and flashing teeth as the dogs caught the scent of new blood and the raw exposed meat. Sweat ran down his forehead as he worked with new desperation, his back bent as he held the beast up to facilitate the knife.

"Martin! go up the bloody hill and see if you can see where those dogs are coming from."
All the while the dog sound grew, seeming to come from all directions at once. Whiti or his boys from the marae, pig hunting, was the most likely possibility. He worked urgently, knowing that if they were as close as they sounded they might pick up the scent of the blood clots, where they lay coagulating in the morning sun, drawing the lazy buzz of blow flies. If they smelt the blood he knew he would have to fight them off the carcass, kill-crazed and passionate as they tumbled random attacks upon the prize. He visualised the arrival of the hunters with leering grins, quickly summing up the scene and knowing they had caught him red handed. Whiti had a way of using such knowledge to his own advantage. They hunted the same patch.

"Well what the hell's going on"?
"It's Jake and Hulme doing a muster"
"Where are they?"
"Its OK, they're down the bottom of the valley riding up towards the green bach."

He smiled grimly with some relief and stopped skinning for a moment, easing his back. Of all bloody days to pick. Jake was the stockman who looked after the cattle that grazed the block and Paul Hulme was the owner. Jake rode around a couple of times a month but Hulme only arrived once or twice a year to inspect his estate. Today was the day and he would ride the more accessible areas checking the cattle and fences.

He pulled the last of the skin from the backbone and yelled to Kathleen for the hand saw. To cut through the spine diagonally he had to pull the top part of the beast forward, so that it sat with its haunches upon the ground, and balance the sides so that they fell away from the saw to the left and right equally. It was heavy work now and the sweat stung his eyes and mingled with the blood and fat which clotted his forearms.

Finally he stopped and rolled a smoke, wiping the blood from his hands with the long grass, still wet from the dew. He was satisfied with the butchering job. The dogs had kept him to good time and now the beast lay skinned and cut into quarters. They could only carry a quarter each, so regretfully they buried one forequarter in the earth, with the skin and guts. The hole wasn't really deep enough, but he stamped the clay over the shallow mound. Hopefully a dog would have to come right over the spot before it picked up the scent. If that happened it wouldn't take long for them to scrape away the earth and reveal the crime. He retraced the flight of the beast, rubbing the coagulated blood drops into the mud with his boots. It seemed the best they could do.

The journey home was difficult but liberating. Still the occasional dog barked from a long way up into the valley. They went by the most direct route, through the steep mānuka and bush covered gully that ran directly down to the cabin. It was slippery underfoot and the great chunks of meat that they carried in packs was awkwardly unbalanced, and sent them at times sprawling forward or back, as they slipped often during the downhill descent. By the time they reached the clearing they were exhausted, hardly able to stand under their loads. Mud patches obscured their worn clothes, which hung damply, cooling the sweat that ran from blood and fat flecked brow. The lumps of meat were still tolerably clean, wrapped in pieces of old sheet before being stashed in the back packs.

He hung the quarters in the meat safe that stood on the shady side behind the house. This meat safe they had picked up off the side of the road and it was still good on three sides but open where it would eventually be connected to the house. He hung the quarters with twine and dragged an unused door from under the house to prop in front of the safe opening in an attempt to close the gap. Being winter the flies were not an urgent problem and the meat only needed to set before they planned to salt it in a large rubbish container.

Throwing off the mud stained clothes they plunged into the cold mountain stream, washing the traces of the kill from work hardened bodies. The stream invigorated, leaving a feeling of exhilarating new life as they became one with the purity of the water and the quiet warmth of the sun. Returning to the cabin the wood stove was lit. They were warm, clean and they had meat. They had succeeded and come home with the kill. A winter's supply of good beef to keep them strong over the wet months ahead. Satisfied and jovial now, Kathleen began cooking the liver with onions on the stove, while he drank hot tea and smoked a joint with Mart. Clouds of euphoria drifted among the smell of cooking and the warmth of the fire.

From the pūriri tree a tui called, celebrating the sun. Stoned reverie recalled the time they had first come to the valley. For only 30 minutes one evening he had stood with Kathleen on a muddy farm track in the rain, gazing upon a beautiful wilderness. A pure sapphire stream, winding through mature native trees and majestic black ponga fronds, cascading from the very heart of Maungataniwha. The blood of the monster mesmerised their hearts, as they gazed in awe at the intense moodiness of the cloud drenched bush, climbing from the valley to caress the sky in every direction. They became one with the miracle of Rangi as he caressed with warm tears the life giving womb of Papa. Somewhere close a kiwi called.

The next morning they had signed the bill of sale without even knowing where the boundaries were. It wasn't boundaries they were looking for, but escape. Escape from the struggle of being born without monetary advantage and the tiresome need to play the system. To take up the dice and advance around the board towards some nebulous state of old age security. The deadening dog trot of insulated, suburban boredom and working for the man within safely prescribed limits. Escape from the synthetic stimulation of a life lived in cemented cages, where it had become too hard to find the umbilical cord of the earth mother. The cord which now lay discarded under several feet of black tar.

Just about the time the liver was almost cooked, these reflections were shattered by the excited yapping of dogs, which accompanied Jake and Paul Hulme as they rode up to the house. They tied their horses to the garden fence and entered the warm cooking smells of the cabin.

Jake was now approaching his eighties and had worked as a stockman all his life. His eyes were red and watery and he was usually unshaven. Being a smoker his emphysema was quite well advanced and he was not able to walk far. He kept his job on the strength of his experience and ability to spend long hours in the saddle. He needed the horses for legs and yet he treated them with a utilitarian harshness. Today he rode Rata, a lazy roan gelding, and raked his sides unmercifully with metal spurs to keep him moving.

Paul Hulme was in his early fifties and not as saddle hardened as Jake. A rounded pastoral face with soft caring manners. A respected member of one of North Canterbury's farming dynasties. Hulme's father had broken in the land and given him a good start, allowing his son the luxury of the speculative life. He still lived in the South Island, where he owned several farms and had come to the Far North some years earlier to buy cheap land. In this block he had bought more than 2,000 acres. Large and beautiful tracts of native bush mixed with rough regenerating pasture. The valley shared boundaries with the state reserve and the fences were poor, allowing the stock to browse free native tucker over the winter. A few years after his initial purchase he had sold off 400 acres, in three blocks, for three times the price he had originally paid for the lot.

Kevin and Kathleen had bought 75 acres from Hulme's original block, but with the latter being an experienced farmer he had inserted a clause that circumvented the normal obligation for him to pay for half of the fencing cost. That meant that now, although they had been there several years, they had as yet only fenced off a few acres around the cabin and Hulme's cattle continued to graze the 75 acres as they always had done.

"What've you got cooking?" said Jake, sitting carefully in the best chair, closest to the fire and the table.
"Oh just a bit of liver," said Kathleen, "would you like some?"
"No, but I wouldn't mind a cup of tea and a bit of your home made bread girl."
He spoke with a wheedling voice and simpering grin, winking at Hulme. Kevin reading behind the facades began to relax and suspect that this was just another social visit. Jake needed a round of tea stops, throughout the day, to help the fags go down and he secured his place at various tables by pissing up the leg of the lady of the house. Kevin sat on the dilapidated couch and made farming small talk with Hulme. Martin, more than awake to the grim humour of the situation, stirred the liver, and winking to

Kathleen suggested a number of times that what Jake needed was a decent feed.

"Actually Paul I had wanted to see you to talk about our mortgage," said Kevin.
"Oh yes," said Hulme, drawing his white fingers together in prayerful mode, like a priest about to begin a session in the confessional.
"Well, as you know we've paid most of it but we still have $2000 to go and I wanted to ask if you would give us a year's extension to finish it off."
Hulme swallowed and averted his eyes, sweeping around the cabin in an attempt to find the right words.
"Well Kevin, as you know, we all have our commitments and its better for all of us that we meet them on time."

Jake coughed to break the silence and invited Hulme to eat from the bread and tea that Kathleen had placed on the table. Martin continued to grin and stir the liver. Kevin shifted from the couch to fill his cup but passing the rear window of the cabin momentarily froze. He saw that several of Jake's dogs had pushed in behind the door of the meat safe and were dragging a hindquarter of beef across the grass, snarling ferociously over ownership.

Without hesitating he moved to the sink and picking up a half full bucket of scraps, excused himself and left the cabin. Outside he moved quickly around the back to the meat safe and with quiet determination began to kick the shit out of the lead dogs. He grabbed the meat and rehung it quickly in the safe and tried to secure the door. The dogs backed off looking mournful and slobbering. As quietly as he could, he abused them vilely, explaining in graphic detail what he would do to the balls of any of them who persisted in such behaviour. The dogs backed off further and he re-entered the cabin.

Inside he looked for opportunities to scowl at Martin and Kathleen, to alert them to the new danger, but they were drifting on euphoric clouds, still inviting the landlord to eat from his own beef routine. Putting the bucket down he began renegotiating with Hulme.

"Well Paul, I'm glad you mentioned commitments. It strikes me that while we've been busy paying the mortgage your cattle have been grazing our land and I thought it only fair that you should pay us something for the grazing."

Jake coughed up a bit of phlegm, to assist his digestion of the bread, while Frank drew his hands together and attempted to smile benignly.
"Well you know that legally the onus is on you to fence our cattle out," illuminated Frank.
"Yes, but that's all just legal bullshit. The fact is that we are carrying about 15 beasts per annum for you and at even fifty cents, per head per week, which would be very cheap, that makes approximately $700 dollars you owe us." This time Hulme coughed up phlegm. Kevin however, wasn't there to hear. He had caught a glimpse from the same back window of the dogs going through a repeat performance. Mumbling something about needing a leak, he quickly headed around the back to the meat safe.

"You bloody son of a bitch!" he began, at the same time aiming a kick straight up the lead dog's arse. In quiet but desperate tones he again abused the dogs and rehung the meat. This time he was worried. He was getting angry now at Martin and Kathleen as he went inside and found them still unaware of the impending doom. He darted daggers at them but they could not see. What about some support you bastards?

"OK," said Hulme,""I'll have a think about what you said and see what I can do."
"Let's go and have a look at the garden," said Jake, wiping crumbs from his stubble and hoping to change the subject. They stood, and with Jake making some final patronising remarks about the quality of the cuisine, shuffled outside. To get to the garden they had to walk immediately past the meat safe.

Discreet subterfuge evaporated as a shaft of sunlight exposed the open doorway. The chemicals in his head instantaneously retrieved a long forgotten file. Kevin reflected in the light of a street lamp, with a white pot of paint and dripping brush in hand. He had just been caught, red handed, by the Principal and Deputy Principal, in the act of desecrating the main glass doors of the Teacher's College. His mate had buggered off, moments before detection and left him with no way out. Instantly he froze, with a lunatic stiffness, imbecile face looking up at the shaft of street light, with the brush dripping white light from his hand. They began to apprehend him, then castigate, and finally to plead but he totally ignored them and with imbecile grin, searched desperately for the source of illumination, like a sculptured DaVinci. Finally embarrassed and discouraged they moved off under the pretext of looking for the others. Kevin hastily became human again and buggered off back to the pub.

Nothing remained now but a brazen return to the theatre of the absurd. Picking up the empty bucket again, he positioned himself alongside Jake, knowing that he was by far the shrewder of the two, and together they shuffled around the back. He was thankful to see that the dogs hadn't yet got back into the meat safe, but hung around, sniffing and slobbering. A few blowflies had also gathered and buzzed expectantly above the doorway. He scowled ferociously at the dogs, which backed off at his approach. Making himself as big as possible he walked sideways, facing Jake, like a partner in a tango desperately trying to obscure his view and keep up a continuous conversation about the garden. Like a good eye dog, he moved the party past the meat safe to the garden gate. Jake and Hulme made a few patronising remarks about the garden as they finally began to mount the horses.

"Got a bit of meat in there," said Jake as he nodded towards the blowflies around the safe.
"Yeah, we caught a couple of eels last night," and their eyes locked.

The three went back inside and thoughtfully ate the liver. In the springtime, when the beef barrel was almost empty, a cheque for $500 arrived. It was from Hulme for the grazing.

The Ruru

It was almost time for the night hunt. Kāha woke from a broken sleep, irritably ruffling his feathers. The machine that had grumbled through his sleep was louder now, roaring angrily as it ascended the slope, puffing sparks and filling the air with its strange scent. Kāha could not yet see it clearly. Shapes even close were still vague. This was the time of haze. The time to awaken and receive the gift of the dark. The time of renewal when the eyes were kissed by night, the mother of perception. Although he had never seen it he knew from the teachings that at this time, Rā the father of light was plunged into the sea.

The machine roared triumphantly as it gained the rise, trampling the mānuka underfoot, clanking and snorting, pawing at the earth and leaving in its wake a geometric pattern of death. Kāha had seen the pattern of its tracks by night. Straight double lines sometimes crossing in confused distortions, but always the same indelible mark of its passing. The machine was close to the pūriri tree now. Kāha could feel the trunk shrink back and tremble as it passed. The noise was deafening. Yes that machine was filled with hate that it would roar its song of death so loud upon the wind. Kāha felt the rage grow within him. He was beginning to see clearly and could make out the shape of the man that rode the machine. He had wondered why a creature as small as the man was not overcome by it until he had noticed that without the man the machine slept. He now realised that although the man was small he exerted a power over the machine guiding its path of destruction. The machine was filled with hate and drew its power from the man who must also be filled with hate. The man rode on top of the machine and together they raged death and fear.

The machine reached its nest, its song regular and throbbing. Suddenly it shuddered and stopped. Kāha looked at the man. Almost clearly he saw him striding towards his nest. The man held the power of life and death over the machine and Kāha now understood that to stop the machine he must destroy the man. For long nights he had sat without food, pondering the meaning of many things, his mind filled with visions. When his mind finally cleared his path was chosen and so tonight he waited for the man.

Last night he had once again hunted to rebuild his strength. After the hunt he had flown to the northernmost point of his territory, the old junction with Pointed Claw. He had sat silently drawing upon the spirit of his friend, already a season past the crossing. He remembered the time before the man. Since the passing of Pointed Claw he was the only one left. The only living witness of the flight from Ranui.

Ranui had been invaded by many men. These men had driven beasts chained together and with the help of these they had attacked the children of Tāne, flinging them to the ground and dragging them away. Kāha remembered the terror of the time when he had crouched, blinded by the day, hearing the rumblings and groaning of Papa, the earth mother, as her sons lay broken upon the earth. Kāha was young then and had left with the strong, a chance to fight for a new territory. The old had remained and he had thought them timid, until now. So he had entered this valley, strong and adventurous. Perhaps it was the violence he had recently witnessed or just the arrogance of youth, but on a cold autumn night he had answered the challenge of Taita the Old. Taita had the best territory in the valley. The pūriri tree that stood high above the cleared place looking down the river. Nightly he called his challenge, defying all.

Even now Kāha smiled grimly as he remembered Taita's surprise. How Taita had called again as though making sure that it was not some mistake, or only his own echo blown back along the valley. Once again Kāha had challenged, so strongly that he knew that only a great warrior would answer. Taita answered, taking immediately to the wing, hot to throw the usurper from the trees. The battle had been long and terrible. Kāha had never known the fury and cunning of an opponent like Taita who had set about his task like an old master. He was ruthlessly fast, knowing exactly when to strike and when to withdraw. Kāha's wounds had been terrible. Most of the scars from his body had come from that night when he had hung on desperately, against all odds, trying to keep moving, using his youth to wear down the other. Somehow he had hung on and bleeding badly it had been he who had delivered the death stroke. In this way Kāha had won his territory, the pūriri tree, the best spot in the valley, where the man now settled.

The man had entered his nest. Darkness had fallen. It was raining lightly and Marama the sister of Rā was thin and already halfway across the sky. The rain came in waves blown from the west. Kāha sat and looked at the nest of the man, waiting. He remembered the time the man had first brought his grumblings to the valley. It had caused a lot of excitement and the nightly calls carried the howls of its progress. Kāha had listened silently with much disquiet. He noted the tone of the calls. So, little brothers, he thought. This beast of man fills you with excitement. Has the good hunting of your nightly rounds become a thing taken for granted? You greet this thing of man's as an interesting diversion. A thing of entertainment. Birth, death and life under the winds and sky are not enough. Not for you the teachings of the night. But alone he had raged, saddened by the decline of the old ways, never joining in the discussions but calling only his challenge to the four directions. Then finally they had come.

Kāha had just dined on fresh mouse and settled back warmly on his return to the pūriri tree. They must have been waiting for him nearby and arrived suddenly, without parley, alighting further out on the same limb. Kāha flew at them. The nearest, a heavy young cock, he gripped with his claws while the other slipped to a lower limb and called, "Te Kāha of Ranui, we mean no harm. We have a message from the circle."
"Then," said Kāha, throwing his captive from him. "You should observe more carefully the old rituals my friends, and if you have come to parley then observe the parley greetings. When you have done this then I may choose to speak with you."

The two flew off and shortly after began the call for parley. Kāha waited awhile. As his rage subsided he smiled at their surprise that he had actually attacked them. There had been a steady erosion of the old customs. Many of the older ruru had slowly acquiesced to the habits of the young, even slipping into the new ways themselves. He called them in and listened to their news. The one he had gripped spoke. He carried a message from Red Eye of the circle. Red Eye requested a word with his old friend Te Kāha and wished to speak with him regarding the recent attack upon the valley. Kāha sat silently long after the messengers had gone, brooding. He had known it would come and now he wondered what they expected of him. What did they think that he Te Kāha could do to halt the progress of the man? He who had retreated once already.

On the night following Kāha flew to the place of the circle. It was a kauri grove. In the branches of the highest tree, the symbol of perception, the circle gathered. Kāha called the parley and was invited to enter. When he alighted, Red Eye and the five other members of the circle were already gathered.
"Welcome old friend," said Red Eye. "We are glad that you have come. No doubt you are aware of the trouble that is among us. There is much fighting among the population as the hunting diminishes and a turning away from the old customs. We have decided that the time has come to move the circle. We wish for those that are able to fly in search of a new place. A place where the old ways can be re-established and the circle renewed. Those that are too old to fight for a new territory will remain and make the best of what is left. We are agreed that you, Te Kāha of Ranui, should go

with the strong and re-establish a community in the old way.

As Red Eye spoke, Kāha had listened silently thinking his own thoughts. He respected Red Eye whom he had known for many years. He also knew that his universal conceptions were crumbling.
"I thankyou," he began after a short silence, "for the faith that you put in me, but I will not accept this task. This task must be given to one who is young and full of optimism. I am now old and my heart is filled with pain."
Red Eye looked at first surprised and then a little angry. "What has happened to the great spirit of Te Kāha of Ranui that he refuses to accept this task. Has he grown soft that he will not do again for the brothers of the valley that which he has already done once so well before. A chance to re-establish the circle, to bring......"
"Friend!" interrupted Kāha, his voice sounding tired and distant. "Where is this place? Where can you go to escape the machines of man? Look my friends. I will not tell you that the circle is forever broken. I will not tell you that to move is futile, or that you do not comprehend the totality of the horror that is among us. I am not the voice of doom to drip cold water on the hopes of others. This is what I say to you. I have spent many nights alone concerned with the quest for perception since I was a regular member of the circle. It is regrettable that I cannot save the brothers of the valley. I am directed down another path and go to answer the call that is the basis of our creed. A man has entered my territory and is building his nest there. This man is challenging my right to a place that has grown with me over many seasons. This time I will not leave. I cannot turn my back on the place like the shedding of feathers. I must answer the challenge of the man."
"But you cannot fight a man. You will surely perish and your leadership will be so cheaply lost to us," answered Red Eye.
"I believe that there is always a way, even though the path may be hard to find and difficult to execute. I go to seek the way. That is my answer."
""What will you do Red Eye?"
"I will stand and fall by the power of the circle," came the reply.
"Then good fortune my friend and farewell."

Three nights later he had been summoned again. Once more he had flown towards the Kauri grove, full of despondency. He had slept only fitfully that day, his dreams punctuated by the sounds of the destructions and the trembling of the earth. The air was alive with despair. A cold wind fragmented the night calls in confused distortions. As he neared the grove he picked up the call of the Kiwis, irregular and piercing, full of fear. Lower came the desperate voices of the Rurus who had territories close to the grove. It sounded as though they wished to leave but lacked direction. Then from high above he saw the bones of the Kauri lying brokenly across

the earth. The highest, the symbol of perception already cut into pieces.
"Where is Red Eye," he asked.
"Red Eye never came out when the destruction began," he was told. Surely he was destroyed?"
"Not destroyed, renewed," said Kāha softly and diving down from the others he swept low over the grove, stopping all others with his call of death.

And that night
the river ran brown
as the spirit of the kauri
ebbed frothing.

Rain
not of a violent storm
the rage of a taniwha

Rain
of a different kind.
Warm, soft and very wet.
The true weeping of a mother for her sons.

The time for waiting had gone. Kāha sent thoughts of the past from his mind as he waited for the sign. Alert now he watched carefully the house of the man. It came. A quick flash of the light, dulling for a moment, then rising in its power, chasing the night from the clearing. Kāha drew himself up and glared hazily at the light. The light that hung from the man's nest nightly, obscuring his best hunting. The light that the man lived by, drawing his power for destruction. The small light that the man burned to keep alive during the night. Destroy the light and you will destroy the man. Destroy the man and the circle could be renewed. Night will follow day.

Kāha drew himself up, filling his huge chest and flung his challenge at the man. Three times he called but was answered only mockingly by the soft hissing of the lantern. He paused only a moment, and then attacked, flying directly at the light. As he came close he smelt its scent, but had no time for reflection as it blinded his eyes drawing him in. He felt a burning sensation in his chest as he connected. The lamp was dashed from its hook and fell with Kāha to the veranda floor, bursting into flame as the glass smashed, spreading the kerosene. Kāha rolled quickly sideways clawing his way towards the grass. He heard the noise of voices and the tramp of running feet. He felt weak and shaken with badly burned feathers on his chest and left wing. Brokenly he flew back to the puriri tree. Watching he heard a loud hiss and the light was extinguished.

Kāha began his victory call, breathlessly at first but building to a song of defiance. As he called he heard the man approach through the dark, staggering and falling over things. "Ah," he thought grimly. "He is already beginning to die," and he called more strongly. Then a deafening noise and Kāha exploding into fragments realising instantaneously that he had begun the crossing.
"Got the bastard," said the man. "Ruined a bloody good lantern." Moving awkwardly through the dark he made his way back to the cabin.

Hunting Pigs

Late in the night a pūkeko shrieked. Silver clouds scuttled across a waning moon. A car door banged them awake inside the house. A bottle rolled out of the opened doorway and smashed on the concrete path.
"Why didn't you ask for the bloody opener if you wanted a drink?"
Cursing followed by muffled laughter.

Mavis, instantly awake, jolted her head from the table.
"Quick you kids. Get off to bed"!
Pushing her bulk from the table with heavy forearms she moved to the couch and shook her daughter awake. The two boys grabbed bleary eyed at a ragged blanket and scuttled towards the bedroom. The daughter began to cry and rubbing her eye smeared tears and snot over her cheek.
"Shut up Bub. Get off to bed"

Wearily picking up Bub she half dragged her to the bedroom and tried to tuck her in at the foot of the double bed.
"Get off!"
Miriama kicked out at the sudden weight draped across her feet.
"Cut that out!" shouted Mavis, thumping a heavy fist across her back. Miriama began to whimper quietly. Stretching out her arm she snuggled into Tui still asleep beside her. Bub finally slipped between the two sets of legs and snivelled into a troubled sleep.

Mavis bustled back to the other room. Smoothing the rumpled cover on the couch she looked furtively through the gaping venetian blind. Light rain split the half-moon into many pieces and the wind erratically twisted the trees in the driveway. Several dark figures urinated in the flax bushes beside the fence. Faint cigarette glows illuminated windswept shouts and drunken laughter. A huddled figure on the other side of the car vomited into the drain. She knew that would be Hori. He was always the drunkest. She let the blind slip and hurrying back into the kitchen turned on the oven.

"Mavis get some bloody kai on!"
Takimoana, her husband, kicked open the door. He carried a crate of beer and a flagon of cheap sherry. These he deposited under the bed by the window and stretched himself out. He was a tall man with a wiry frame. Instinctive like the wild pigs he hunted. Narrow, quick eyed face that alternated engaging good looks and cruel anger. His moods intense like summer thunder. Tonight she saw that he was ebullient, bubbly like the

froth at the top of the bottle. Uncle Henare came in, a huge framed man with a relaxed smile. He half carried Hori, who looked pale and shrunken. Kevin, a pakeha hippie from up the valley, brought a guitar. Her oldest son John followed. John was 18 now and had begun drinking with the men. He carried the smouldering coals of explosive fire in his belly. Work hardened shoulders, like bacon hams, rippled with reckless strength. He waited his time to settle the score with his father. Finally Takimoana's young nephew Hemi, carrying another crate, followed with his pakeha woman, Cara.

Ah Cara. Cara had arrived unexpectedly from the city only a month ago. Large breasts bursting out of her tight blouse. Shapely legs all the way up to the short skirt that snapped tantalizing glimpses of gaudy panties. Full sensuous red lips parted lightly in a sly smile as though she was thinking something unrevealed. But those eyes! Full dark lashes and deep brown pits focused slightly down and away. As though she knew what they were thinking. As though she found the suggestion attractive. In the males of the whānau she excited sidelong glances. Furtive erections of desire that turned away, intimidated by the force of her feminine sexuality. In the men she raised a question.

Tonight she sat on the bed, resting lightly against the legs of Takimoana who was making a fuss of her husband, carefully filling his drink and his ego. Hemi was easily led, a weak, friendly person who rose to the bait of his own importance. Takimoana laughed loudly at his jokes and entertained them all with tales of bravado.

"You should have seen this bugger this morning." He pointed to his son John. "First of all we had to walk all the way to the fence line to get the tractor."
"It was alright for you man. I had to carry the bloody diesel. All you had was the tucker bag," grumbled John. Takimoana ignored him.
"When we got there the damn battery was flat. I told John to hop on and give it a jump start."
"I noticed you weren't offering." John tried again.
"No fear it was too bloody steep for me mate. That's why I told you to get on." Takimoana laughed his mischievous laugh, shrill and mocking like the pūkeko.

"Anyway, this silly bugger gets on the tractor and puts it into gear. Off he goes down the hill with me and Henare up the top pissing ourselves laughing. As soon as he lets the clutch out the bloody back wheels lock and the tractor goes into a slide. You should have seen this bugger leap over

the side and roll head over heels into the gorse. Off down the bloody hill the tractor rolls, arse over tit to the bottom of the gully. We pissed our selves laughing. Next thing it starts to pour down with rain. Bugger this we thought. It doesn't seem to be our day. So we buggered off back to the pub. Henare reckons, we won't go back until the boss gets the tractor back up to the top of the hill or wait a few bloody days and hope it rains like hell."
"It's alright for you, you bastard. Next time you'll be on the bloody tractor."
Takimoana laughed loudly and filling Hemi's glass moved his leg so it rested casually against the thighs of Cara.

Through the night the party spluttered and danced from shadow to shadow, flickering indiscriminately like a candle blown without thinking. Shrieks of hilarity echoed the wakeful periods of the pūkekos squabbling in the swamp. Mavis sitting in the kitchen joined in the merriment with well practiced timing, keeping a careful eye on the moods of her men. She sat in the chair beside the door that led into the children's room. She heated the food and coaxed the men, trying to bully the visitors to eat, knowing that most wouldn't bother until the beer was gone.

Before the candle burned out one of the good plates crashed to the floor as a body slammed into the outside of the house. John had followed Hemi outside and smacked him in the side of the head. Hemi staggered heavily back against the wall of the house as John advanced, screaming obscenities. Henare and Kevin staggered outside and standing between them calmed John down. Takimoana took the opportunity of the unexpected turmoil to caress Cara's buttocks. Slightly drunk she began to purr and flicked a strand of hair from a flushed face. She looked at him. He smiled at her with intent, watchful eyes.

The others came inside from the dark with John still swearing and angry.
"Shut up boy and fuck off if you can't take your piss," shouted Takimoana. John, glaring, red eyed, turned away, not quite ready yet.
"Come and get your tea," defused Mavis.
"Yeah get your tea boy," said Henare gently. John backed off, saving face and staggered off to his damp caravan out the back, spilling the last of his sherry over his bush shirt as he slipped backwards off the step. Uncle Henare drove the others blearily home.
"Sleep in that room nephew," Taki indicated to Hemi the second room where the younger boys slept.
"Mavis, make up the couch for Cara."

Cara, lying quietly, heard the sounds of her husband snoring in the other room. She had not drunk much. Her intoxication came from drinking in the furtive looks of desire. Among the men she felt her power. In her presence they jostled to be noticed. Tonight the one all the others deferred to had placed her in the centre. His flashing smile and lithe strong body mirrored an earthy knowing that complemented the coarse bush smell of him. Being the leader of the pack he was used to taking what he wanted and this animal wildness excited a challenge. Unlike the sophisticated veneer of her city conquests his eyes of desire unleashed a curious passion. Deeper mysteries of her source were suddenly open and exposed under the fragmented candle light. Just like the others, her own man looked on weakly, accepting feigned affability to screen his helplessness. Even he wasn't that stupid but she knew she could take the risk, for Hemi would have her on any terms, whenever she allowed him. Humiliation fired his lust and made him more compliant. She liked this throne of vanity upon which Takimoana's brutality had thrust her and fanning the fire in his eyes she led him forward.

Now, as Takimoana had engineered it, she lay on the couch, only half a room away from where he feigned sleep on his bed under the window. She saw him rise. A dark form illuminated by a pale fragmented moon, whispering nice words in her ear and gently pulling back the blanket. He slipped an electric hand inside her blouse and stroked her breast. Sherry and tobacco breath caressed her ear, sliding across her cheek to fix passionately on her mouth. Hot, wet and urgent, he kissed her lips, fumbling blouse buttons open, resting his hand momentarily on her navel. She strained her body forward pulling him over her.

"Taki get out of there, you bastard!"
It was Mavis. Hands across broad hips. Blue eyes burning with disgust as she stood her ground, to be degraded no further. Passionate in defence she grabbed Taki by the shirt and yanked him sideways off the couch. Like an abused dog he rolled to his hands and knees, swearing weakly under his breath but moving back to his bed, knowing that this wasn't the time. Cara lay abandoned and shamed. As the pūkekos crept from the swamp in the first light of dawn, Mavis catnapped fitfully, seated uncomfortably on the armchair between them.

A week later the sun withdrew behind the hill in a blaze of extinguished glory, the pink mingling with the greys of the evening. Yellow fires turned slowly red. Smoke from the camp fire spiralled lazily skyward, unmoved by the wind. Faintly a Ruru warned of the night. Dogs squabbled over the bones of the morning's hunt, while the boys brought the horses up from their afternoon tethering under the trees. Mavis, bent over the cooking fires, yelled instructions to the girls and younger boys. The men were seated under a tarpaulin erected among the trees, on the piss again. Cara sat in the centre, close to Takimoana who entertained Hemi with pig hunting tales.

"This bloody pakeha fella came up from Auckland. Reckoned he had the best dogs in the north. Bloody top bred Rhodesian Ridgebacks that cost heaps. He asked to see our best dogs so we showed him Missy."
Taki whistled low and several dogs gave up their squabbling and approached the edge of the group.
"Look at her. Just a bloody mongrel."
Missy was small, rounded and multi-coloured. Deep scars lined her muzzle and flanks and she tried vainly to wag a broken tale.
"She's only got three bloody teeth in her head but we've caught more pigs with her than any dog we ever had."

"Remember the time we had that big boar backed up into a hollow log," contributed Uncle Henare. "We thought it must be a big one the way the dogs were hanging back. So we grabbed Missy and threw her into the log. Next minute all hell breaks loose and this huge boar comes barrelling out of the log with bloody Missy up on its back, hanging on to one ear. Dogs were going in all directions until Takimoana steps up and lets the boar have a shot gun in the side of the head. A pellet must have gone through Lady's tail and it's been hanging like a bloody frayed rope ever since."

"We watched that poofter from Auckland drive out the next day with nothing. He made out he didn't see us," laughed Taki. "We'll take you out later tonight Hemi and get you a good pig."

Later that night some solid rain set in. The men still sat, intoxicated, under the ragged edges of the tarpaulin. The fire burned brightly and a few plates of smoked eel lay about. With the last of the sherry gone it was time to make good the boast of the hunt. Takimoana was drunk but still with his wits about him. No way was he too interested in getting soaking wet that night for any bloody pig. He knew exactly where to go to find a good boar early next morning when he sobered up. Now he had the boys hanging around in the rain on wet horses, waiting for the men to finish drinking. He also had the boast to Hemi, and he had Cara very much in mind.

"You boys take the dogs and ride up around the top side of the hill. If you get on to anything it will run down the creek out to the river flat. We'll wait there."

The boys knew too much to be overly impressed with the plan but being glad to be moving, rode off up the stream bed in the thick rain, laughing and trying to startle each others horses in the dark. The men took a couple of single barrel shotguns and followed Takimoana with Cara and Hemi down towards the river flat.

Takimoana walked through the dark feeling the way with his feet. He relied on the blueprint in his mind of what the country looked like in the light. Cara followed close behind; reaching out to him in the dark, amused at the cheeky way he stumbled against her with drunken caresses. Hemi followed some way behind with a flashlight, good wet weather gear and a shot gun, excited to be finally doing it. Others followed behind, slipping occasionally, laughing and staggering.

After hanging about the river flat for a while, checking the eel lines to fill in time, they listened for sounds of dogs barking up the hill. Takimoana then decided he had to split the group.
"Can you hear that dog barking, boy?" he said to Hemi.
"Yeah," said Hemi, wanting to sound onto it.
"You take your shotgun down and wait at the entrance to the gully. That's the most likely place for a boar to come down. I'll go up a way and make sure it doesn't run up the other side."
"I think we should all stay together," replied Hemi, who couldn't see an inch in front of his face.
Bastard, thought Takimoana.
"Well, alright boy. Lets all move up there."

Takimoana set off quickly in the dark, grabbing Cara's hand and pulling her with him. Cara, knowing what he was up to followed excitedly, abandoning herself to the moment. He turned quickly from the entrance to the gully and moved diagonally across the hill into the bush. Cara followed, sliding and banging into him when he slipped, catching his feet in supplejack vines, or sliding down invisible banks in the darkness. She held onto his belt, completely lost, having to trust in him to find the way. Feeling around the slippery roots of a large tree, she unexpectedly stumbled, sliding head first down a leafy bank. Rising up she realised she was alone. No belt to grip onto and she couldn't hear him near her. She stopped, listening. Panic waves swept over her as she paused, turning from one side to the other.

She thought she heard a voice, off down to her left where the others had been. She took hesitant, quick steps in that direction. A piece of bush lawyer gripped her thigh. She struggled sideways feeling the prickles break her skin and draw blood. She lost her footing and slid several metres against the base of a ponga tree. Face down she smelt the decaying leaves. Mud covered the back of her skirt and she felt the wet soak through to her skin. Her raincoat was saturated and dripped through, wetting her blouse. She felt too foolish to call out. Standing again she decided to head downhill, half walking and slipping on her buttocks, or tripping and rolling over exposed tree roots. Crashing against a low branch she pulled herself upright catching her breath. She listened. Nothing but the drip of the rain through the trees and the muffled weight of the impenetrable blackness.

She eased the cut of her panties where they had pulled into her crutch and smoothed the muddy skirt down. Taking another step the ground suddenly gave way beneath her. She plunged over a vertical mud slip, crashing into the rocks and entwined tree trunks of the creek bed. She lay still a moment, sucking in the air with startled gasps. Her leg was stretched awkwardly under and she was covered in wet clay. One foot dangled in a large pool in the creek. She felt a boulder against her head.

Then the boar came. In a series of grunts, he staggered lightly through the undergrowth. He smelt the panic in her erratic flight. The helplessness that could not deny him. He pulled her out of the creek and lay her on a flatter bed of fern. He felt the heat of her body where her skin dripped wetly. He pulled open her blouse and grasped her breasts, bending to kiss their dripping ripeness and heard the pounding heart. He sensed her fear as she clutched at him. She wanted to be held and comforted but instead felt repulsed by his forceful insistence as he pushed her again on her back wedging her legs open to him. She started to cry as he entered her. Meekly she lay with face turned upwards to the heavy rain drops splashing from the leaves as he ejaculated with powerful thrusts, grunting and groaning. Finished, he collapsed on her, panting.

Back at the campfire Mavis watched them as they came in. Cara red eyed and shivering. Wet mud still on her skirt and raincoat as she hunched beside the fire. Hemi sat subdued to one side of her. Takimoana drank from his last stash of sherry, staggering about and laughing uproariously at his own jokes. Tripping on the fierceness of drunken power. Mavis took a hot drink from the pot and gave it to Cara. She turned and stood directly in front of Taki with hands on hips. He faced her swaggering.

"You dirty bastard Takimoana."
He burst into drunken laughter, derisively mocking.
Mavis moved back to the fire, angrily stirring the stew for tomorrows breakfast.

Sometime early in the morning, as the red streaks of dawn stabbed at the dark clouds, a pūkeko shrieked. Takimoana darted in beside Missy who hung on grimly to one ear. The boar hesitated in panic a moment. He grasped the foreleg and flipped it on its back, pinning its head to the ground with his boot. With a savage grunt he plunged the knife deep into its throat so that the blade pierced the heart. The boar violently convulsed, ejaculating the last of its blood onto the sodden leaves of the forest floor.

The Murupara Gig

It was raining. Heavy drenching rain that mocked the futile attempts of the windscreen wipers to fling it aside. Rain that drummed authoritatively on the roof of our vehicles, searching for any weak points and slowing our progress to a crawl as the small convoy wound around the road to Murupara.

Through a globular screen I peered ahead, eager for my first view of the gateway to the Tuhoi tribe. The Children of the Mist was the tribe that had stood resolutely with Te Kooti during the land wars. Avoiding conquest they had melted into the steep bush clad gullies of the Ureweras, hidden by the forest that nurtured them. What the soldiers could not do by force, time had achieved through dogged persistence. Peering from among the ferns the Children of the Mist caught glimpses of the good life and would taste her. Today Murupara is a forestry town and the people laid the axe to the forest replacing it with exotic pine. Through the tears of Rangi, the Sky God, I glimpsed a pub and a fish and chip shop, well lit as we drove into the car park of the local hall.

The sound boys, being keen to set up our 2,000 watt p.a. system, backed the covered trailer up to the entranceway and began to unload. Inside the hall several Māori kids bounced a basketball, and shot at goal while the only adult in sight approached me.
"Oh you're the band that's come up from Tauranga. Well you're wasting your time. These kids won't listen to you; all they want to do is play basketball."
"But we were asked to come up here and play for your youth group?"
"Yeah, I know but you're wasting your time. We've had some of the top names in the country come up here and none of them have done any good. The kids don't listen to them. Anyway, wait till Hiko comes, he's in charge."

By the time Hiko came the sound boys already had half the gear unloaded, trying to be oblivious to the basketballs that whistled perilously close. I envisioned balls through bass bins and horns crashing from the top of eight foot stacks. It turned out that Hiko was no more encouraging than the first bloke.
"These kids just won't listen to you," he said.

This piece of information completely outraged the sound boys. I mean after all someone had invited us to play this gig and having driven all the way up here, at our own expense, it looked as though we might not get the chance to express ourselves. Sound fanatics they might be but nobody was going to take them for idiots.

I pacified the troops and then went back to talk to Hiko. "Listen man, it seems we've been caught in the process of poor communication but seeing as how we're here we might as well do something. Personally I don't care if we perform our thing or not. Maybe we could play basketball with the kids?"

Hiko thought that one over. "I'll tell you what, out the back there's another room about the size of a double classroom. Why don't you set up out there and then those who want to can come in and listen, while those who want to play basketball can play."

After some serious discussion this compromise proved acceptable even to the sound boys and they began setting up a greatly reduced system in the back room.

I went back to talk with Hiko who gradually began to open up.

"We have no control over these kids. When our church began this youth night six months ago the behaviour of the kids was staggering. A few of them even came in and urinated on the floor of the hall while some of the older ones got drunk and copulated out the back. Someone left faeces smeared under the seat. I told my helpers not to say anything. We have to love these kids. Some of them just get belted or neglected at home, but we have to treat them as Jesus treated us. We accepted them. If they smashed the wall we fixed it and if they urinated we mopped, but we never complained. One night a drunken teenager came at me with a knife. I prayed aloud in the name of Jesus and he just folded up in the centre of the floor and cried. After that they gradually began to change. Now they don't do those things anymore, in fact if any trouble-makers come in the kids sort them out because they like coming here. But we still can't make them do anything. Usually they just want to play basketball. At least it provides a place for them to go while the adults are at the pub. They probably won't listen to you." I left Hiko and sat quietly in a corner for a while. It was my job to front the show.

Meanwhile in the back room the younger locals had crowded in to teach the sound boys a thing or two. Cheeky little Māori kids, checking out the amplifiers, wanting to carry speakers and roll out leads. There was nothing they didn't know about bands.

"My uncle's got an amplifier better than that one. He can play the guitar good too. Once he was on TV."

"We had a better amplifier than this one but it got left out on the veranda one night and the goat ate the front out of it. Dad nailed it to the wall to keep the plates in."

I was relieved to see that the sound boys were enjoying themselves. Back block Māori kids bubble over with an enthusiastic innocence and a quick humour that can win the hardest hearts. They disarm you, until you stand face to face, now, in the present. The who you are, naked and perceived.

Eventually we were ready. We stood before all the younger ones, a swarm of eager faces yelling out and cracking each other up with their cheeky antics. Most of the older ones remained outside, playing basketball or just hanging beyond the door.

"Well what do we start with?"

The band looked at me. I looked at the kids hoping for inspiration. I remembered a conversation I had had with our lead guitarist at the start of the tour. He was a professional musician from way back and had toured NZ many times with a lot of the top names in NZ show biz. He told me that when they played Māori pubs they found that if you could play guitar boogie fast, then you were right. I remembered the truth of that from my own days in the rock band.

"Guitar Boogie," I said picking up the bass,""Fast!"

We hit it hard and by the time we were halfway through some of the older kids slipped inside the back door. Next we did some 12 bar blues with harmonica and jazz flute. The basketball stopped and the rest slipped quietly in.

I never worked so hard at playing a gig like I did that Murapara gig. You could lose them within half a song so I watched their eyes, stalking their attention, with all preconceived show formats out the window. Finally we got onto our major piece which combined both music and drama and showed the history of man from the fall to the restoration. As the snake entered the garden they hissed and jeered warning against the bite that robbed them of their heritage. At man's futile attempt to cover themselves with a fig leaf, they laughed uproariously. Then a sombre brooding silence as they watched humanity pass from localised drunkenness and violence to global holocaust. Stomping and shouting they joined with those who called for the death of the Saviour, but wept under the pain of the lash, and would have reached for a sponge to mop the bloody brow. A standing ovation as death turned to victory at the saviour's return, to restore mankind with his gift of love. Once again the forest grew.

After we had packed up I found Hiko mopping out the muddy foot prints in the foyer.

"You did well," he said. "They listened."

"They only listened to us because they watched you."

We drove out of Murapara under a sullen sky, but the rain had stopped. The tears of Rangi, absorbed by the mop of love.

Milk Cow Blues

"Kevin! Get that fucking cow off the road!"
A quiet morning in late autumn. Scattered clouds gathering enthusiasm for another shower. The kingfisher, busy working the morning river is momentarily distracted from the search. An engine revs and the sound of boots as MacCartney strides forward swearing at the cow.
"I'll get the county to put this fucking cow in the pound!"

Kevin puts down the hammer and walks to the edge of the half built wall. Looking across the river flat to the road, he can see the ute and the large bearded figure of MacCartney gesticulating angrily. He says nothing. Reaching into his pocket he sits on the ground and rolls a smoke. Silence. MacCartney slams the ute door and drives up the valley. It is some moments before the kingfisher calls and the river song permeates the violation of engine noise.

Drawing on the smoke, his annoyance sucks from deeper pits. How many acres are needed for escape? No matter how far you go the suburbanised arseholes follow, trailing their usual baggage of regulated power trips. Before MacCartney he had roamed free, with no one between him and thousands of acres of pristine bush. Now he heard the annoyance of small machinery nagging on hot afternoons. The dull throb of the generator, inhibiting the love songs on warm ruru nights. One of the main pig hunting trails cut off.

And the bloody cow - for fucks sake. I mean like, it's really only a bloody farm track. Each evening he locked the calf in the small milking enclosure and turned the cow out the gate to eat from the grass along the sides of the track. Some of the grazing was quite extensive with pockets of rich swamp and pasture between the road and the nearest fence. The cow was quiet and very happy with the arrangement, browsing richly throughout the night and never failing to return to the yard to be milked in the morning. Kevin needed to conserve the grass that he had fenced for the winter. That bloody cow should be paid by the county for keeping the roadside clear.

But what do you do?
MacCartney had arrived noisily, six months earlier, confidently outlining his plans to make money by felling kauri trees from his bush block. The river he would dam to make electric power to run his tools and the milking shed that would enable him to milk goats that would also clear up the scrub and

rubbish areas. Even his shed would be bigger than the house that Kevin still worked on and eventually he would have a large octagonal house built with the native timber that he intended to fell. Three months ago he had clanked up the track in a hired bulldozer and laid paths to the largest kauri trees, despite the impassioned protestations of a few hippie settlers. The trees once felled turned out to be rotten in the centre. Not enough money there.

Kevin had not gone to protest that day as the hippies made him uncomfortable. He had sat alone at home, when later that day it rained, warm impassioned tears, as Rangi wept unashamedly for the spirit of his departing children. The river ran brown with the dirt bulldozed aside.

Now of course the road would have to be widened and metalled so that MacCartney could get his vehicles in and out, to get the salvageable timber to the mill. And no bloody cows in the way to halt the trucks of progress. Three times over recent weeks MacCartney had strode angrily, calling his challenge across the river. Kevin had not yet answered.

It had become unfashionable to fight in these parts. The hippies breathed marijuana clouds of peace and love. The men wrapped patterned lava lava's around their waists and baked wholesome bread with the delicate sensitivity of women. The women dressed in overalls and dug in the gardens without shaving their legs or armpits. Not for them that old-fashioned macho definition of roles. These were sensitive, liberated people, drawing from Eastern gurus of acceptance and being. Sometimes though, he noticed that the men fought like women and never spared the sharp word behind the hand to anyone who hadn't accepted the light. The hippies were often educated, middle class people who had dropped out of society, in the sure knowledge that if the going got tough they could always pop back to pick up a good job or comfortable inheritance.

His drop out track was working class based. Tumbling up amid the passionate, violent outbursts of a poor suburb on the outskirts of Dunedin. An Irish, Catholic dog, that stank like a frog, was often the subject of physical attack from the numerically superior Protestant Scots. The green cap, worn like a label, made altercations hard to avoid and some days he just had to stand and defend himself, or the younger ones of the family. He was urged forward by the encouragement of his mother, who flashed boundless courage, bred from a positive spirit, well tempered by the necessities of fate. And what did you do, she would ask tauntingly, probing for any sign of weakness. She seemed to know that his first instinct was avoidance. That he preferred to drift sideways. Yet he had some confidence in knowing, that when pressed hard enough, fear became the motivator that made him utterly uncompromising in attack. Like a cornered rat he reached a state of calculated fury and went for the kill effectively.

The kingfisher cut through sparks of iridescent sunlight to alight on the branch. With powerful gulps it swallowed the fingerling trout. Preening itself it drew to its full height and began to call. From the boundaries of its territory an echo sounded. Kevin stubbed out the smoke and stood up. So today was one of those days. A day on which the challenge had to be answered. Something deep would not let him turn away any longer.

His horse was still tethered with bridle along the fence from the early morning hunt. He could hear Kathleen working in the cabin. I won't tell her, he thought. Her attitude would only annoy him and make him double minded. She thought all the men were overgrown boys squabbling for territory in the sandpit. It annoyed him that she couldn't understand that sometimes in life it was for real and also that she didn't appreciate the resourcefulness he usually exhibited in handling sometimes precarious situations. When she did react it was with courage but poor judgement. She just hadn't had enough practice.

He looked for his boots and laced them carefully. I might as well be standing on a firm foundation, he thought. Rolling a final smoke he looked around the yard, hitched up his trousers and then climbed into the saddle. He smiled as he heard Kathleen talking to him, not even realising he had gone. With calculated detachment, but very conscious of the bright, early autumn morning, he rode up the road towards MacCartney. He thought he would probably be working out the back on his boundary and that's where he found him. Coming down the hill, off the ridge towards the river flat, he could see him working on the fence near his Landrover. MacCartney started and called out a blustery greeting. What sort of bastard is he, he reflected. Could he forget the performance with the cow so quickly? He didn't answer and just rode unhurriedly up beside the Landrover.

"MacCartney, what's the bloody idea of hassling my cow?" he said with quiet determination. MacCartney went right off. His face burst into impetuous anger as he stamped and began to shout a tirade of foul abuse, finally blurting out in crescendo,
"If you weren't on that fucking horse, I'd break this bloody batten right across your fucking head!"

Kevin was angry now. That chemical thing had been touched off. Climbing deliberately out of the saddle, he led the horse the short distance and tied it to the landrover. Walking back he stopped an arms length away and looked full in the face of MacCartney. He was a big man, at least a head taller, with broad shoulders and a full beard. After a silence he said quietly,
"I'm off the bloody horse now MacCartney"

With surprise he watched a look of growing panic sweep over the face of MacCartney.
"No! No!" he stammered, "I'm not a fighting man," and he dropped the batten. Looking bent and fearful he began shambling backwards. Kevin seasoned his anger with disgust.
"You loud mouthed bastard MacCartney. You're just an arsehole!"
Angrily he strode after him, shouting insults until MacCartney turned and finally ran, beyond shame, up the fence line.

Kevin stopped, a wave of pity sweeping over him. Poor pathetic bastard. He went back to the horse and rolling a smoke, calmed down as quickly as he had fired up. He waited. After a time MacCartney began walking back down the hill talking about fencing and farming in an over shrill, wheedling voice. He felt a wave of disgust.
"Listen MacCartney. Just cut the bullshit. Leave my bloody cow alone. Here's my hand, you can have it either open or closed."
With a dawning realisation of escape and a return of confidence, MacCartney accepted the hand and began to turn on Mr Nice Guy. Kevin looked him in the face hard and then mounted and rode away.

Gutless bastard, he reflected. Obviously always got away with bluffing because he was big. Never had any practice at the real thing because he wasn't called out enough. Just bullshit and bluster. He felt exhilarated riding quietly back down the track in the full, late morning sunlight. Returning across the stream he noticed the kingfisher, at rest, relaxing iridescent head across buff slumbered chest.

He aint Heavy- He's your brother.

It was almost midnight. Black waves slip-slopped heavily under the pier. Patches of mist shimmied in waves from the lamp posts. A shadow broke from the pōhutukawa tree and approached, moving into the light. A Māori in his late twenties, hunched and unkempt with the hesitant stagger of a drunk. I reached for the heaviest spanner I could feel in the tool box.
"Is this your car?"
Yes this was my car. An old Holden, growing tired and beginning to choke the plugs with oil. Under the light of a street lamp I cleaned them with a wire brush in preparation for the twenty kilometre drive home.
"Take me to the Hihi turnoff bro?"

Take me to the Hihi turnoff bro! Yeah sure thing bro. I've been up half the night at a band practice and now I'm cold and tired and wanting to go home to bed and you just asked me to drive off fifteen kilometres in the opposite direction. And by the way Bro, one of the things I've grown to hate most in life is messing about with cantankerous drunks. But then I remembered. Give to everyone who asks you, and if anyone takes what belongs to you, do not demand it back..... If you love those who love you, what credit is that to you.....?
"Ok bro. I'll take you to the Hihi turnoff."

His name was Tanerau. He seemed to know me and I recollected seeing him on the fringes of the local drug scene. Tanerau was a nobody. A man of little mana. A fleeting shadow that was occasionally caught in the light that reflected from other men. Now he sat, shoulders hunched, caught on the bad side of a bender. The cold stretch under the tree had begun to sober him, with the awful realisation that there was nothing further to reach for. No marijuana or booze to dull the pain and only that painful dawning awareness. Gradually the warmth of the car brought momentary relief and he began to relax and talk about his fight in the pub and what a tough guy he was. Truth was the pub had sucked him dry, and when he became a nuisance some of the boys smacked him over and threw him out onto the pier, just above where the effluent pipe discharged its excrement into the sea.

"I was sitting in this car bro, before you came along."
"What! how did you get in?"
"Aw, I know how to get into these cars. Matter of fact I had it all hot wired ready to start up. I was going to drive myself home when something

stopped me and I thought you can't rip off this car. This is Paddy Coogan's car. So I sat waiting for you by the tree."
So it's not good enough for you to rip off my car, you'd rather waste my time and have me chauffeur you home in the middle of the night. I began to like him. It seemed my mana was still ok with the local boys because he knew they would have given him a hard time if he'd stolen my car. I considered also my habitual prayer when I had to leave the car parked near the pub.
"I'm glad you didn't. See, you didn't have to steal it, all you had to do was ask."
The words came a bit forced, for I remembered the hand that reached for the heaviest spanner in the tool box.

I approached the Hihi turnoff with a dawning uneasiness. I couldn't remember any houses at the turnoff. I looked for a light. Maybe somebody was going to meet him there. No waiting car. I drifted slowly to a stop.
"Take me home bro?"
Take me home bro! A further ten kilometres down some of the windiest road in the county. You sucked me in bro. I began to like him more. I considered that I could just throw him out here, but I drove on.

The drive to Hihi was slow and meticulous, as the old Holden negotiated the narrow road. Mist obscuring in waves but occasionally breaking bright and clear as though a shroud had been lifted. Tanerau in the front seat, sometimes loud and loquacious, talking of himself and those we both knew. Alternatively hunched and silent with not even a cigarette to hold onto as the waves of drunkenness receded. Finally we arrived. Surf crashed desolate upon a midnight beach contrasting the silent darkness of Tanerau's house close to the sea.
"Come in bro!"
Yeah I thought, I'll come in bro and enter the dark secrets of that house. Never mind the others who might be lurking with evil intent or your own mood swings. I'll come in because something has brought us here and seems as yet incomplete.

Nobody else was home. He staggered about the kitchen and placed some stale biscuits and a cup of tea without milk before me. We sat facing across the table, and then he tried it.
"Give me a joint Bro!"
"I don't bother with that stuff anymore mate."
"I heard you stopped. You don't drink now either. Eh?"
So I told him about it.

Tanerau listened, pale and intent, dishevelled and lost. Then he told his story, with tears melting his tough guy face. As a defenceless child he had huddled under soiled blankets while his father smashed his mother against the kitchen cupboards. He was force fed beer in his bottle to keep him quiet during the long drunken nights. Now himself a man he watched the love of his wife and child drift through pity to contempt as he lay grovelling in his own blood and vomit. A month ago they had left. Last weekend Tanerau tried to reach them, promising again a sober life. When he arrived in Auckland he was drunk and after causing a scene at her relations place was eventually thrown out. Driving back he wrote off his car and two others on the Auckland harbour bridge, adding a huge debt to the millstone already round his neck.
"I love them bro but I can't stop. My father poured it down my throat."
"Who's pouring it down your throat now bro?"
"What, but I can't stop. Pray for me bro."

A seabird rose above the surface of the waves. The fingers of a silver dawn turned black to grey. An engine started down by the beach. Tanerau on the step, watching the headlights clear the darkness from the corners of the road. Cold but elated I drove home.

You can't go wrong with a hāngi

One warm Saturday after lunch, Sean snapped awake to hear Glenn say, "I'll put down a hāngi!"
Through the fog he ascertained that they had decided to invite a group of Samoans down next week. Funny, he hadn't connected Glenn with hāngis before. Then he remembered that Glenn's mother was Māori and although Glenn was a redhead, he had a flat nose with flared nostrils. Up until then, he had always considered it the result of a bar room brawl. He made an instantaneous decision that it would be a wise move to help Glenn out the back with the hāngi.
"Good idea, I'll give you a hand."

On the Saturday morning Sean got up nice and late, had a leisurely breakfast and gave Glenn plenty of time to get organized. With his son Bernard, he arrived at Robert's house, as it started to rain. There was no sign of Glenn. He quickly scouted around and saw half a dozen river stones stacked in a pile with a few lengths of mānuka. Hardly enough to dry your socks with he thought. Robert saw him and pounced.
"That bloody Glenn! That's the last time I'll ever trust that bugger to do anything. I should have known better."
"Steady on mate," Sean counselled, "we've still got time."
"Yes but we've got 80 people to feed and all this meat. How are we going to cook it? Maybe we should send it round the people's houses and get them to put it in their ovens. But we've hardly got time for that. That bloody Glenn."

"Well look, hang on mate, give him a chance to turn up and we'll make a start. We can still get it down in enough time as long as he turns up with the gear."

Fortunately, Sean had done a few hāngis years ago, so he had a rough idea. He knew that if they started the fire immediately, they still had a chance of meeting the deadline. The spot that Glenn had picked looked good. An old patch of garden, nicely tucked out of the weather between two plastic houses. Bernard and Sean started digging the hole. When this was finished they raided a pile of fruit tree boughs that Robert had stacked for the winter. With the mānuka it began to look like it was just about enough. It was raining heavily now when Glenn pulled up in his ute.

"Gidday!" I see you dug the hole." He came up grinning broadly.

"Yeah, well we thought we'd better make a bit of a start. But like I told you, it's a long time since I've done a hāngi. How's it looking?"

"Yeah, it looks alright, yeah," he reckoned, walking around and unloading vegetables and wire baskets off the ute.

"No, you can't go wrong with a hāngi, mate. I've always wanted to put one down."

"Hang on, are you telling me that this is the first hāngi you've put down?"

"Well, I've seen a lot done at Mum's place," he laughed,""but we'll be right, you can't go wrong with a hāngi, mate!"

"Well I hope so mate, because if we don't get this tucker cooked we'll both be up crap-street. Robert's not too happy, have you seen him?"

"Yeah," reckoned Glenn,""When I drove up he stomped off in the other direction."

They organized the fire as best they could and heaped up the river stones. It didn't look quite enough so Sean suggested they swipe some of Robert's landscaping rocks. It was pretty solid rain by now so they got some diesel out of the shed and began to douse the fire.

"That might taint the meat," reckoned Glenn.

"Well better than eating it raw. Anyway if the buggers are going to die then they'll want a good feed first."

Feeling more relaxed now that things were finally under way, they yarned and joked as they sat around peeling the vegetables.

"Is that fire on a bit of a lean," reckoned Glenn, after a while. Getting up to have a look they noticed it had burnt rather quickly down one side and as they discussed the probable causes, it collapsed, shrugging its burden of hot stones to the ground.

"Bloody hell!" reckoned Glenn, scurrying about quickly looking for the shovel. With some difficulty they began re-stacking the burning faggots and lifting the hot stones back on top of the fire.

"That looks better," said Bernard with some relief, as they thrust blistered hands into the cool of the vegetable water.

"No worries mate," laughed Glenn. "You really can't go wrong with a hāngi, as long as you get the rocks hot and keep the sacks wet."

"Where are the sacks?"

"Hell!" said Glenn. "I forgot to ask. I'll tell you what, how about you and Bernard keep an eye on the fire and I'll shoot around to my cousin's place."

A crack like a pistol shot interrupted him and they turned again to the fire. As they watched, a flaming meteorite exploded skywards. At the apex of its gravitational flight it faltered, showering incandescent cosmic sparks all over Richard's plastic house.

"Bloody hell!" said Glenn,"'what was that!"

Before they had time to reply two more went off in quick succession.

"It must be those landscape rocks."

"Quick get them off," said Glenn, "before Robert comes out."

Scurrying again for the shovels, they stoked the fire and began knocking the stones off the top.

"Watch your head," said Glenn, as another went off, and lurching to one side, he slipped in the mud falling flat on his back. Bernard and Sean's frenzied laughter rapidly turned to desperation as cascades of sparks continued to shower the plastic house. They jumped about, swearing and sliding until with some heroism they managed to knock the landscape rocks off the fire and re-stack it. Sweating and blackened they once again rested their hands in the vegetable water.

"Right, well you fellas should be right for a while. I'll shoot off and get the sacks," said Glenn.

Sean and Bernard finished the vegetables, then cut up the meat and filled the hangi baskets. Nothing to do now but wait for Glenn and keep the fire piled up nice and compact. They alternated hot and wet as they turned slowly before the fire in the rain. An interminable time later, Glenn finally showed up with some sacks, looking slightly flustered.

"My cousin didn't have any sacks," he explained. "So I shot round to the neighbour's next door. The bugger wasn't home so I grabbed the sacks out of the shed anyway. Do you reckon those stones will be hot enough?"

They stood in the rain peering at the rocks in an educated way.

"I know," said Glenn. "You do the spit test." He spat. The spat spit sat coagulating on the rocks, without a hiss of steam.

"No good," he said. "I'll tell you what mates. We're going to have to get a bit more mānuka."

"Where are you gonna get mānuka," Sean queried.

"Oh we'll just grab your chain saw and get a few bits off the side of the road. Like we do up north," said Glenn.

"Hey mate, pardon me for stating the obvious but we ain't up north," reminded Sean. "'This is the posh, lifestyle block area of Drury."

"Come on," said Glenn. "We've got to get those rocks hot."

Sean grabbed his chainsaw and leaving Bernard to hold the fort, they roared out the gate in the ute. Despite Glenn's muttered protestations that the bloody country was full of mānuka it seemed to Sean not to be the case. While there were a few patches growing along the sides of the roads, they were always in full view of one house or another, and as they drove around they just couldn't seem to shake the burgeoning city.

"Bloody hell," said Glenn. "Up north the stuff springs up everywhere. I know lets try the reserve up the top of the hill."

Glenn stopped the ute by a two acre public reserve, beside a cemetery. Sean could see at least four houses silently watching from where he sat.

"You realize there'll be a hefty fine if you get caught cutting native out of there?"

"No! we'll be right," said Glenn. "Look mate, all we're doing is getting a couple of bits of mānuka for a hāngi. The bloody country's full of the stuff." Glenn grabbed the saw. Sean knew they had to go all the way now. Those fifty hungry Samoans had to be fed.

"Right then."

Glenn strode purposely towards the cemetery with the saw. No sooner had he reached the fence than an angry tirade stopped him dead.

"What the hell d'ye think yer doing in there!"

A fiery old Scotsman strode angrily towards them from the house at the bottom of the hill.

"We just wanted a bit of mānuka for the hāngi," remonstrated Glenn, with some bluster

"If yer cut one bloody stick from there, I'll call the cops an ye'll spend the next six months payin for it. Now bugger off!"

The Scotsman strode so determinedly towards them that even Glenn's optimism evaporated. Throwing the chainsaw back in the ute, he jumped back into the cab and drove quickly.

"Who's bloody country is it," muttered Glenn, "All we wanted was a few sticks of mānuka."

As they drove rather dejectedly back to Robert's, they noticed a small grove of mānuka with several dead limbs fallen across the fence.

"No one will want those," said Glenn,"'let's go in and ask." He swerved into the gate and stopped before a rambling old farm house . Glenn bounced out and knocked on the door. An elderly Dutchman stared through the doorway and listened impassively. He eyed them suspiciously.

"Vat mānuka.. Show me. I vil come down."

With growing confidence Glenn explained about the hāngi, the spit test and the fifty hungry Samoans as they walked down the fence line.

"Vitch one do you vant," he hissed. "'OK! you can have this one, and this one." Without further ado Sean started cutting, while Glenn raced back for the ute. They cut the two limbs the Dutchman said, and two others by mistake, given that the chainsaw drowned out the protestations. For good

measure they grabbed a couple more bits which lay in the grass. The Dutchman stared after them shaking his head as they roared off.
That mānuka burned beautifully. The rocks passed the spit test, and by the time the first of the Samoans turned up, the tucker was nicely covered, under the dirt, out of the pouring rain.

"Now listen!" Sean found himself counselling the ladies in the kitchen. "Just explain that lunch will be a little bit late. Put out plenty of drinks and chippies and we'll serve the kai as soon as possible. Keep them happy."

Three hours later they stood looking at the sodden dirt heap by the plastic houses.
"I hope the bloody thing's cooked," muttered Glenn, poking his finger in the dirt searching for heat. "Shall we leave it another half hour?"
"Listen mate, me and Bernard have just come back from our final diplomacy mission in the kitchen and the mood is turning rapidly sour. They are bloody hungry and we can't hold them any longer. That thing comes out on the dot of three hours and if it's not cooked, I'll be in the car and out that gate faster than an exploding rock. Let's do it."

Gingerly they grabbed the shovels and scraped away the dirt. They were pleased to see steam puffs seeping through the sodden sacks. They pulled back the layers and examined the first basket. The meat looked alright. Feeling more confident Sean and Glenn took a side each and walked hopefully towards the tables. They dumped the basket on the carving table among a bubble of hungry Samoans and pulled back the last sheet. The meat was so beautifully cooked it just fell off those bones without a knife. The fifty Samoans ate their fill of the best hāngi Sean had ever tasted and the good humour of the gathering was instantly restored.

"Told you," said Glenn.
"You can't go wrong with a hāngi mate." He was sitting in the ute just inside Robert's gate. As he started the engine, a Holden pulled to a stop throwing a flurry of stones across the driveway. A Maori fella jumped out running at Glenn.
"Hey! did you break into my shed and pinch me bloody sacks mate!"
"See ya," said Glenn, and hastily engaging the gears he skidded across the footpath and roared off in a northerly direction.

A Grey Faced Smiling Suit Man Said

Or at least I thought he said

A political force
Of benign dimensions
Has conjured a sum of money
For the purposes of solicitous allocation.
With discrete nod and wink
it will assume a guise of progressive change
to win friends and influence many.

As you would indeed expect
we have appointed a departmental directorship
to allocate the money
with a perpendicular motion.
Freely we will give to all those who
fulfil the prescribed criteria
which will at present remain concealed
in a congealed, vaporous mist.

The sum of money being precariously ill defined
shall remain tantalizingly nameless for a time.
Like the programmes
which we hope it will cogently stimulate
In an effort to meet
your needs
and their needs
and our needs
Because at the present time
It's what we need.

We have performed this collaborative consultation,
collectively and quietly hoping,
that our quintessential motivation
will define the problem for you all.
Such direct and forthright leadership
in sending a pragmatic allocation
disproportionately through the nation,
gives cohesion to us all

I didn't know what to say.

Glossary

Constans Fidei	Latin inscription on the Coogan family coat of arms. "Be constant in faith."
Hāngi	Māori oven of heated stones covered with earth.
Kererū	NZ native wood pigeon
Kōhanga Reo	Literally a language nest. Name given to Māori pre-schools which teach the language.
Koru	A spiral pattern. The spiral on the fern that unravels and becomes a new leaf.
Kōwhai	Native tree with yellow hanging flowers which the nectar eating birds love.
Mānuka	Flowering scrub plant that acts as nursemaid to other native species by providing shade. Very good firewood.
Marama	The moon.
Maungataniwha	Maunga means mountain. Taniwha can be a mythical dragon-like being. It can be good or bad. It can refer to a Māori ancestor who becomes a Taniwha after death. It can be a tribal guardian. A spiritual caretaker of mountains, lakes, streams etc. A taniwha is a wonderful powerful force.
Miro	Native tree that has autumn berries which the Kererū love.
Mokopuna	Grandchild. Can be male or female.
Mullet	A very good eating fish that inhabits tidal estuaries.
Papa	Short for Papatuanuku the earth mother.
Ponga	A fern tree
Pūkeko	Blue-black swamp bird about the size of a hen that shrieks in the night.

Pūriri	Beautiful spreading native tree that provides flowers and berries for Kererū and tuis.
Rā	The sun
Rangi	Sun or sky. The male spirit that cohabited with Papatuanuku to give birth to the creatures and plants in our world.
Rata	Red or white flowering native tree that begins life as a scrubby bush.
Ruru	NZ native owl.
Tāne	Tāne Mahuta the god of the forest.
Taniwha	See Maungataniwha.
Taonga	Treasure
Te Ariki	Is a paramount chief. Loosely translated as Lord. In a Christian sense could refer to God or Jesus.
Te Kooti	A chief of Ngāti Porou who became one of the most successful guerrilla fighters in the land wars against the British
Tekoteko	Usually refers to the carved figure on top of a Māori meeting house which normally represents a Māori ancestor placed on the meeting house to ward off evil.
Te Reo Tikanga	Means customary language. The correct use of language.
Tui	A beautiful native bird with a silk ruff under its throat. It is the warrior of the bush and one of the sweetest singers in the forest.
Tūrangawaewae	A place where one has the right to stand on ones feet and speak.
Whakapapa	Genealogy
Whare	House

Recent and forthcoming titles from ESAW:

Tiger Words
Paekakariki Poets $10

Music Therapy
Peter Olds (poetry) $15

the smell of oranges
Jill Chan (poetry) $15

The Sun is Darker
Jonathan Fisher (poetry) $18

Dumber
Mark Pirie (poetry) $15

The Singing Harp
Iain Sharp (poetry) $15

The Road Goes On
Brian E. Turner (novel) $35

Travel and other compulsions
Heather McPherson (poetry) $18

To . . .
Bill Dacker (poetry) $15

Bookmarks
Winter Readings at Arty Bees Bookshop $15

They Drank Kava
Moshé Liba (poetry) $15

The Estuary of Komo
Moshé Liba (poetry) $15

take a seat and rest awhile
Rosalind Derby (artwork and text) $25

Only a bullet will stop me now
Niel Wright (poetry) $15

Also available:

Toku Tinihanga: Selected Poems 1982 to 2002
By Michael O'Leary
Published by HeadworX $20

Plus:
Toku Tinihanga
a CD featuring Michael O'Leary with music by Trevor Bycroft and Blackthorn. Recorded at Waimea Studios, Christchurch,
for ESAW (Sounds Division) $20

Greatest Hits
An Anthology of writing from ESAW and HeadworX publishers $30